ACCOUNTING THOUGHT AND PRACTICE THROUGH THE YEARS

Edited by Richard P. Brief

A Garland Series

A NEW APPROACH TO MANAGEMENT ACCOUNTING HISTORY

H. Thomas Johnson

Garland Publishing, Inc.
New York and London
1986

For a complete list of Garland's publications in accounting,
please see the final pages of this volume.

The articles and papers in this volume are reprinted with the permission of the
journals, editors, and publishers listed in the table of contents.

Accounting, Organizations, and Society is a publication of the London Graduate School
of Business Studies.
The Accounting Review is a publication of the American Accounting Association.
The *Business History Review* is a publication of the Harvard Graduate School of
Business Administration.

Library of Congress Cataloging-in-Publication Data

Johnson, H. Thomas, 1938–
A new approach to management accounting history.

(Accounting thought and practice through the years)
Includes index.
1. Managerial accounting—History. 2. Managerial
accounting—History—Research. I. Title. II. Series.
HF5635.J654 1986   658.1'511   86-9956
ISBN 0-8240-7865-9

Design by Bonnie Goldsmith

The volumes in this series are printed on acid-free, 250-year-life paper.

Printed in the United States of America

For Elaine—with love

CONTENTS

PREFACE

Before the 1970s historical studies of management accounting had an extremely narrow focus: they ignored almost completely the internal accounting practices of actual business organizations. Their indifference reflected two common misconceptions. In the first place, accounting historians considered management accounting to be merely a peripheral consequence of the financial reporting process. In the second place, they regarded the published works of accountants as the only sources they needed to consult for their investigations. Accounting historians were limited, too, by their conviction that all accounting was a technical process one could study exclusively in terms of itself. Before the 1970s, then, historians of management accounting were inclined to ignore the records of organizations that used accounting. Today we recognize that management accounting is actually an integral feature of organized economic activity. It is not dependent for its existence on demands for financial information made by capital markets. It is not thoroughly and infallibly presented, furthermore, in the published writings of accountants.

The traditional approach to management accounting history that prevailed before 1970 has been brilliantly articulated by A. C. Littleton, S. Paul Garner, and Sidney Pollard. Their work, often referred to in the articles reprinted in this volume, is ably summarized by Michael Chatfield in A History of Accounting Thought. These traditional writers agree that management accounting originated in the need for product costing. Product costing, a financial accounting procedure for attaching costs to products, is necessitated by the requirement to value inventories at cost. They also agree that management accounting did not develop until fixed costs in industrial organizations became large enough to force managers to give attention to accounting allocation procedures. It therefore came considerably later, they say, than financial accounting.

The articles and papers reprinted in this volume, all written after

1970, represent a departure from the earlier conventional notion of accounting history research. They approach the study of management accounting history by regarding the accounting and business records of actual organizations as indispensable source materials for historical analysis. Analysis of these records has yielded a new conception of management accounting. New studies conclude that modern management accounting evolved in American industrial firms long before anyone had a need for financial reporting information. These studies suggest that the forces contributing to management accounting's development are more numerous and complex than historians had realized.

The articles and papers brought together in this volume have been divided into two sections. The first section contains articles offering case studies of three firms operating between the 1840s and the 1920s. These case studies trace the historical development of virtually all the internal accounting practices associated today with management accounting. The second section consists of articles and papers that interpret the case material. They examine recent positions offered by several different accounting historians, as well as scholars in other fields. The issue of how to investigate, and of what to conclude, about management accounting is presently receiving increasingly close and sophisticated attention from scholars outside accounting. It is to be hoped that these investigations and the studies reprinted in this volume will challenge future accounting historians to identify and explore the social, cultural, and organizational forces that shape management accounting.

ACKNOWLEDGMENTS

The idea for this book was suggested by Richard P. Brief when he presented me with the Academy of Accounting Historians' 1981 Hourglass Award. The award was made for a "series of articles on the history of management accounting." Except for the Arthur Young Lecture delivered at the University of Glasgow, the papers brought together in this volume had been written before, and were recognized by, the Hourglass Award. I am grateful to Dick Brief and to Garland Publishing for the opportunity to collect these materials in a single volume. I also thank the editors of *Accounting, Organizations and Society*,

Accounting Review, and *Business History Review* as well as the University of Glasgow's Department of Accountancy for permission to reprint previously published material. Three items published here for the first time include my 1980 presentation to the Third International Congress of Accounting Historians in London and comments by Richard DuBoff and Fred Bateman on a paper that I presented at the 1974 Annual Meeting of the American Accounting Association (the paper itself, *sans* comments, appeared in the July 1975 issue of the *Accounting Review*). I thank professors DuBoff and Bateman for giving permission to reprint their comments in this volume.

I would like to acknowledge every colleague and student who has assisted my venture in accounting history since 1970, but to do so would take more space than my friends at Garland will allow. The following list includes the names of those whose help has made a decisive difference in my work: Alfred D. Chandler, Jr., was the first person to suggest that I explore accounting issues in business history, and he has been a constant source of support and encouragement; Richard P. Brief, S. Paul Garner, Gary John Previts, and Stephen A. Zeff welcomed me into the guild of accounting historians and have continued ever since to provide invaluable advice, criticism, and assistance; the late Robert Lord was a brilliant, energetic man whose ingenious ideas I sorely miss; Anthony Hopwood has helped my work in more ways than I can list in this short space, but his influence begins to appear only in the last two articles reprinted in this volume; Elaine Bowe Johnson has not only rewritten virtually every sentence that appears in this book, she has provided ideas and advice at least as important to me as those that an earlier generation of American writers attributed to the legendary Max Perkins.

I. Historical Case Studies of Management Accounting

Early Cost Accounting for Internal Management Control: Lyman Mills in the 1850's

By H. Thomas Johnson

Reprinted from

THE BUSINESS HISTORY REVIEW
Volume XLVI Number 4   Winter 1972

By *H. Thomas Johnson*

ASSISTANT PROFESSOR OF ECONOMICS
UNIVERSITY OF WESTERN ONTARIO

Early Cost Accounting for Internal Management Control: Lyman Mills in the 1850's*

❦ *This study of the accounting records of a mid-nineteenth-century New England textile enterprise sheds new light on the emergence of modern cost accounting as a specialized tool of management.*

4

Very little research has been undertaken in the accounting records of industrial firms during the period 1840 to 1890 when manufacturing cost accounting emerged as a specialized tool of management control. Several useful and interesting theses regarding the evolution of cost accounting practice have been suggested by business and accounting historians; generally speaking, such theses are rooted in the study of published sources. Alfred D. Chandler, Jr., for example, has indicated that the small-sized, functionally unspecialized firms typical of American business around 1840 were served adequately by the double-entry mercantile bookkeeping procedures introduced almost 550 years earlier. Such firms did not require the statistical data and the cost accounting methods familiar in the modern enterprise. Chandler has concluded that the need for modern cost accounting arose only after 1850 in railroads and after 1870 in steel, chemical, and metal working industries where oligopolistic markets, complex production processes, and problems of large scale organization combined to create a high degree of uncertainty and risk. Firms in these industries needed reliable cost data to determine prices, to assess the results of operations and to evaluate capital-intensive technological innovations.[1]

Business History Review, Vol. XLVI, No. 4 (Winter, 1972). Copyright © The President and Fellows of Harvard College.

* The research upon which this paper is based was financed by the Canada Council (research grant S69–1548) — the help thus received is gratefully acknowledged. I wish to thank also Mrs. Eleanor Bishop and Mr. Robert Lovett for assistance with the textile company records at Harvard's Baker Library; Professors Kevin H. Burley, Alfred D. Chandler, Jr., and Basil Yamey for their advice in the preparation of this article; and Dr. Elaine Bowe Johnson for editorial advice.

[1] Professor Chandler's comments on the emergence of cost accounting are found in his following works: *Strategy and Structure* (Garden City, N.Y., 1966), 174–185; *The Rail-*

Accounting historians who focus on the more specialized, narrow issue of bookkeeping methods similarly argue that modern cost accounting practice did not evolve before the late nineteenth century. They point out that ordinary mercantile double-entry bookkeeping methods were adequate for the external nominal and financial transactions of merchants and traders. These methods did not, however, supply manufacturing firms with data on the results of internal "transactions" involving the transformation of raw inputs into finished and semi-finished goods. Consequently, many early industrialists estimated manufacturing costs on an *ad hoc* basis, using records and scattered memos that did not form an integral part of the firm's double-entry bookkeeping system. The complete integration of cost and commercial accounts that characterizes modern cost accounting could not be achieved until accountants learned how to handle, in the double-entry form, nonpersonal and manipulative transactions (e.g., transferring materials from one process to another and allocating overhead).[2] Progress in the development of the technique was slow. Most accounting historians cite as the earliest example of complete integration of cost and financial accounts in a double-entry system, an accounting text published in 1887.[3]

5

Clearly the integration of cost and financial records was necessary to the development of modern cost accounting as an important tool of management control. Indeed, one accounting historian has described the transition from mercantile accounting to manufactur-

roads: The Nation's First Big Business (New York, 1965), 98–100; *Pierre S. du Pont and the Making of the Modern Corporation,* co-author Stephen Salsbury (New York, 1971), 128–135; "The United States: Evolution of Enterprise" (unpublished ms., September 30, 1970), secs. II and III.

[2] Notable examples of the extensive literature on this issue written by accounting historians are: A. C. Littleton, *Evolution of Accounting to 1900* (New York, 1933), chs. 20 and 21; David Solomons, "The Historical Development of Costing," in D. Solomons, ed., *Studies in Costing* (London, 1952), 1–36; and S. Paul Garner, *Evolution of Cost Accounting to 1925* (University, Ala. 1954), ch. 2. The orthodox view on cost accounting in the mid-nineteenth century was stated succinctly by Paul Garner in his article, "Highlights in the Development of Cost Accounting," in Michael Chatfield, ed., *Contemporary Studies in the Evolution of Accounting Thought* (Belmont, Calif., 1968), 216–17: "During the decades 1820–1880 little can be found which is of interest in the development of cost accounting. . . . The absence of striking innovations is rather peculiar, since many lines of industry were rapidly gaining headway. . . . It is likely that most manufacturing firms simply modified the then familiar trading account to take care of the factory charges. The ordinary goal was, therefore, the derivation of an interim profit figure rather than the cost of production. Almost no firms had worked out the details of how to show the product flowing from one account to the other on the general ledger." The cost records of Lyman Mills which are described herein present a considerably different view of mid-nineteenth century cost accounting than the view which Garner outlines.

[3] The text is Emil Garcke and J. M. Fells, *Factory Accounts* (London, 1887). Garcke and Fells' cost system is described in Littleton, *Evolution of Accounting,* 348–353. Paul Garner states that the Garcke and Fells book "probably had more to do with the advancement of cost accounting practices than any other book ever published. [One of its most striking features was] the procedure for integrating the costing with the financial accounting. This matter had either been ignored, or vaguely mentioned, by previous authorities." See Garner, "Highlights," 217–18.

ing accounting "as an achievement second only to the original development of bookkeeping according to double-entry principles." He states further that the adoption of modern cost systems in industrial practices marked "the expansion of bookkeeping (a record) into accounting (a managerial instrument of precision)."[4] It is unfortunate, therefore, that scholars appear not to have given more attention to early illustrations of firms which adapted double-entry bookkeeping to the needs of industrial cost accounting. In his classic study of accounting history published in 1933, A. C. Littleton noted the paucity of literature published between 1820 and 1885 on cost accounting.[5] S. Paul Garner, commenting over twenty years later on this dearth of studies, also noted that historians interested in the evolution of cost accounting practice have done very little research in nineteenth-century company records. Indeed, it seems that all of the company studies and business histories which have appeared since the early 1930's omit discussion of how industrial firms adapted mercantile bookkeeping to the needs of modern industrial accounting.[6] This gap in the literature of accounting history can be partially bridged, however, by research in the accounting records of nineteenth-century industrial firms. Although such records are scarce, an examination of those available sheds considerable light on manufacturing accounting practice during a period hitherto ignored by accounting historians.

One excellent illustration of an advanced cost accounting system in use before 1860 is provided in the papers of the Lyman Mills Corporation, a cotton textile firm incorporated in Boston in 1854.[7] During the nineteenth century the company maintained its head office in Boston, operated several waterpowered cotton mills along the Connecticut River in Holyoke and sold its finished goods through a commission agent in New York. It is of course conceivable that Lyman Mills was in advance of its competitors in developing a relatively sophisticated cost accounting system at this time. All the available evidence suggests, however, that Lyman Mills was a "typical" firm in the New England cotton textile industry from the viewpoint of manufacturing, output, marketing, and its switch to "fine" varieties of fabric after the Civil War.[8] This is to suggest the

[4] Littleton, Evolution of Accounting, 359–360.
[5] Ibid., 350.
[6] Garner, Evolution of Cost Accounting, 76–90.
[7] These records, housed in Baker Library at the Harvard Graduate School of Business Administration, are described in Robert W. Lovett and Eleanor C. Bishop, List of Business Manuscripts in Baker Library (Boston, 1969), 38. In the following notes, these records are referred to as "Lyman Collection," with the Baker Library manuscript index reference given.
[8] For historical information on the company's operations see Lyman Collection, A–2

possibility that Lyman Mills' records examined in the following pages may not be unique and that further research in the records which exist at Harvard's Baker Library and other archives may yield comparable results.

The importance of Lyman Mills' records is twofold. First, they contain the earliest example discovered to date of a completely integrated double-entry cost accounting system and suggest that such a system may have been used widely, long before historians had supposed. Secondly, although Lyman Mills falls outside the oligopolistic type of enterprise which Alfred Chandler links with the emergence of modern cost accounting, we nevertheless find a price-taking enterprise such as Lyman Mills (possibly also its many competitors) adopting what appear to be similar accounting practices. It is platitudinous to reiterate the differences between a textile firm situated in a highly competitive market in an industry with relatively stable technology and organizational patterns and the oligopolists which Chandler says introduced the modern practice of cost accounting. Our primary objective in the following pages is to examine the cost accounting system in use in Lyman Mills after 1856. Secondly, it is our aim to suggest that cost accounting had a function in the middle of the nineteenth century which differs from that linked by Chandler with "big business."

The basic accounting records at Lyman Mills date from 1856. These include a double-entry general ledger and sub-ledgers which were kept by the treasurer at the home office in Boston, as well as a double-entry factory ledger with related inventory, payroll, and production sub-ledgers which were kept by the mill agent in Holyoke. Reciprocal entries in the home office and factory ledgers were kept current by means of daily correspondence between the treasurer and the agent. The Holyoke factory ledger includes accounts for current assets, current liabilities, and all operating expenses. The factory ledger also includes two accounts (referred to as "mill" accounts) which resemble modern work-in-process control accounts. One of the mill accounts was charged with manufacturing costs related to coarse goods production and the other mill account was charged with manufacturing costs related to fine goods production. The Boston general ledger includes not only all the accounts kept in the Holyoke factory ledger, but also additional accounts for plant and equipment, capital stock, long-term liabilities, and profit and loss. Sales and non-manufacturing expense figures were entered

7

(inside front cover) and Constance M. Green, *Holyoke, Massachusetts: A Case Study of the Industrial Revolution in America* (New Haven, Conn., 1939).

only in the general ledger, where they appear in the two mill accounts. Every six months, the books were closed to determine profit and loss.[9]

The two mill accounts were the keystone that supported the manufacturing cost system in Lyman's books. Every accounting period, each mill account, one for coarse goods and the other for fine goods, was charged with its respective share of cotton, factory labor, and factory overhead expense. These charges to the mill accounts were transferred from separate control accounts for cotton, payroll, and overhead. For cotton, the largest single item of expense, the mill accounts were charged at the end of a six-month accounting period with the cost of raw material that had been used in production through the weaving stage. "Cost" was based on the contract price of cotton, including freight and insurance charges, and was calculated semi-annually (after inventory-taking) on a first-in, first-out basis.[10] Payroll charges were distributed to the mill accounts monthly in accordance with a daily record from each mill that shows employee hours for every process (e.g., picking, carding, spinning, warp weaving, weaving, etc.).[11] Factory overhead was distributed to each mill account semi-annually according to several criteria such as floor area, number of looms, and the rated horse power of water turbines.[12]

The treatment given to unexpired costs in work in process was more sophisticated in the case of cotton than in the case of factory payroll or overhead. In other words, the cost of cotton that was purchased but was either still in transit, or in bales, or in process up to the weaving stage was charged to inventory and not to current manufacturing expense. The entire amount expended each period on manufacturing payroll and factory overhead, however, was charged to the mill accounts, although a portion of those expenses should have been allocated to work in process. This failure to charge unexpired factory labor and overhead costs to inventory naturally caused profits to be understated in one period and corres-

[9] Lyman Collection, CA (general ledger) and CB (factory ledger).

[10] In some years, particularly after 1887, the balances in the general ledger cotton accounts were written down to market when market values fell below original cost. These write-downs were charged against profits in the general ledger in the year affected, but were not recorded in the factory ledger.

[11] Lyman Collection, LC and LT.

[12] Lyman Collection, AM (overhead distribution sheets in the semi-annual accounts). Depreciation of manufacturing plant and equipment does not follow modern practice. Expenditures for plant, equipment and major renovations were generally charged to profit and loss in the general ledger in the year they were incurred. Such charges were not entered in the factory ledger and therefore did not affect the data in the company's cost of manufacturing statements (see below). Ordinary repair costs, however, were included in the overhead expense total.

pondingly overstated in the next. Since the amount of work in process to which these unexpired costs would have been assigned did not change much from one period to another, the net distortion between years because of this practice would have been small. The combined amount of factory labor and overhead was, moreover, a much smaller part of total manufacturing cost than the cost of cotton, which was accounted for properly. The total production cost charged to the mill accounts each period approximates quite closely, therefore, the amount designated as "cost of goods manufactured" in modern manufacturing accounting systems.[13]

Although the amounts charged to the respective mill accounts for cotton, factory labor, and factory overhead are identical in the general ledger and the factory ledger, only the mill accounts in the factory ledger resemble modern work-in-process control accounts. Unlike work-in-process accounts, the Lyman general ledger's mill accounts contain entries for non-manufacturing expenses and sales in addition to entries for manufacturing expenses. Consequently, the mill accounts in the general ledger resemble those early nineteenth-century trading accounts which Littleton and other authorities describe as the "bridge" between mercantile bookkeeping and modern cost accounting.[14] These accounts provide profit and loss data useful in determining the semi-annual dividend to shareholders, but they do not serve management needs by providing direct information on manufacturing costs. The mill accounts in the factory ledger, however, are charged only with manufacturing expenses and therefore give direct data on production costs as a regular part of the double-entry bookkeeping cycle.

It is notable that regular reports summarizing the data from these various cost accounts provided Lyman Mills' management with useful information on production costs. One kind of report, a "cost of manufacturing statement" which gave a *pro forma* summary of labor, cotton, and overhead charges, was prepared from each mill account every six months.[15] These reports include: labor cost incurred in picking and carding, spinning, warping, and weaving; the cost of cotton used in manufactured goods; and manufacturing overhead charges. The sub-totals for each of these three classes of expense, as well as the total óf all expenses combined, agree with the amounts charged to the respective factory ledger mill account. These semi-annual statements on the cost of manufacturing give a

9

[13] Additional information on the transactions in these mill accounts will be supplied to interested readers on request.
[14] Littleton, *Evolution of Accounting*, 325.
[15] Lyman Collection, MAE (semi-annual).

detailed breakdown of the items in overhead cost, such as starch, fuel, supplies, and teaming. They include, furthermore, data on the cost per pound and per yard of output for each major item of expense. Lyman's accountants also prepared *monthly* cost of manufacturing statements which include all the same data as the semi-annual statements, except that the breakdown of overhead costs is not given.[16] These accountants obtained monthly information on actual labor costs from payroll sub-ledgers. They could not ascertain actual cotton and overhead costs, of course, until physical inventories were taken; normally physical inventory occurred every six months. The total cotton and overhead costs included in the monthly manufacturing statements were therefore calculated by applying estimated costs per pound to the number of pounds of goods manufactured during the month. Figures indicating the pounds of goods manufactured could be obtained from mill production records, and the figures on cotton and overhead cost per pound were taken from the latest semi-annual cost of manufacturing statement. If one makes the reasonable assumption that cotton prices and overhead rates did not change much during most six month periods, then one may conclude that, without having to take physcial inventories, Lyman Mills had useful estimates of total manufacturing costs at monthly intervals. Indeed, the monthly cost statements augmented Lyman's regular bookkeeping system by providing reliable aggregate data on production cost more promptly than the factory ledger itself.

In addition to producing these aggregate cost data, Lyman Mills also produced periodic information on the unit cost of each cloth style which it manufactured. Although actual unit cost calculations before 1886 are not found in the documents that now remain, the raw data needed to estimate product costs appear in the company's records as early as 1875.[17] Basically, unit cost was based on the average weight of the yarn in each style of cloth that was manufactured. The weight of yarn that was manufactured was readily available in daily production records. The main problem in costing was to determine the cotton, labor, and overhead expense per pound of yarn. It was very easy to determine the cost of cotton, the most important element of cost, since it was accounted for on a cost per

10

---

[16] Lyman Collection, MAE (monthly).

[17] Lyman Collection, MAF (1886) and MAH-1 (1875). This method of estimating unit costs probably was not described in published sources before the late 1890's. See, for example, William G. Nichols, *Methods of Cost Finding in Cotton Mills* (Waltham, Mass., 1899), 8–18; and James G. Hill, "Various Systems of Computing the Costs of Manufacture," *Transactions of the New England Cotton Manufacturers' Association*, 67 (October 5–6, 1899), 132–37.

pound basis. It was more difficult, however, to allocate labor and overhead expense among the various styles. Basically, the average labor and overhead cost per hank of yarn was calculated every six months; that average cost was multiplied by the number of hanks per pound ín each style to get an estimate of the labor and overhead cost per pound.[18] These calculations enabled the company to estimate total cost per pound for each style produced every six months. It was a simple matter to convert the cost per pound figures to cost per yard. The mechanical accuracy of these unit cost calculations was checked by multiplying the estimated unit cost per pound figures by the total pounds of each style produced every six months to arrive at an estimate of the total cost of goods manufactured. The last figure was then compared with the total cost recorded in the plant ledger mill accounts. The difference was never very great, usually less than 3 per cent of total cost in the mill accounts.[19] These product cost statistics, calculated semi-annually at Lyman Mills at least as far back as 1886, are probably less accurate than those one might get from a modern textile mill's process cost accounting system; however, they gave a reasonable idea of relative cost differences between styles and of changes over time in unit costs.

Clearly, the various cost statements described above were superior to the *ad hoc* memos usually pictured as typical of early nineteenth-century "cost accounting." The dàta in Lyman's statements were drawn directly from the company's ordinary double-entry books of account and provided systematic and reliable information on the company's manufacturing operations. Although the statements do not deal with some items of expense, notably depreciation and unexpired conversion costs, in a manner which we would consider appropriate today, certainly these technical shortcomings should not obscure the remarkable efficiency of Lyman's total cost system. Although Lyman's definition of profit and loss does not correspond exactly to the modern concept, the profit and loss figure in Lyman's general ledger was, nevertheless, tied in to the manufacturing cost data in the factory ledger mill accounts. Such a "tie-in" permitted the management frequent and useful analysis of manufacturing costs and profits.

In conclusion, let us turn to the use made by Lyman Mills of their relatively sophisticated cost accounting system. The evidence provided by the available records gives no indication whatsoever that

11

---

[18] One hank equals 840 yards of yarn.
[19] Lyman Collection, MAF.

Lyman Mills used the data thus obtained in the way or for the reasons suggested by Alfred Chandler for the large-scale enterprises which he studied. In other words, Lyman Mills did *not* use cost accounting to evaluate production decisions or to determine the costs and benefits of technological innovation. Indeed, the firm's book values for net investment do not permit meaningful measures of overall rate of return, since capital investments were charged to surplus as rapidly as possible. Nor is there any indication that Lyman's management ever considered calculating return on investment. Similarly, there is no evidence to suggest that they used their unit cost statistics to assess output levels of various styles in the face of changing market prices. As with most textile firms of the period, Lyman's management focused its attention inwards on the shop, and not outwards on the industry. All the evidence examined points to the conclusion that Lyman used its elaborate cost system to facilitate control of internal plant operations: for example, to assess the physical productivity of mill operatives; to assess the the impact on operations of changes in plant layout; and to control the receipt and use of raw cotton.[20] Although used primarily to rationalize internal control, Lyman's cost accounting procedure antedates by thirty years a system which until now accounting historians have regarded as the earliest example of a completely integrated double-entry cost accounting format.

[20] Lyman Collection, PA and PB. For example, see letters from the treasurer to the agent dated December 8, 1884, February 4, 1885, February 19, 1885, May 23, 1885, November 13, 1885, and April 7, 1886 (PB–14 and 15).

Management Accounting in an Early Integrated Industrial: E. I. duPont de Nemours Powder Company, 1903-1912

By H. Thomas Johnson

Reprinted from

THE BUSINESS HISTORY REVIEW

Volume XLIX Number 2   Summer 1975

By *H. Thomas Johnson*

ASSOCIATE PROFESSOR OF ECONOMICS
UNIVERSITY OF WESTERN ONTARIO

Management Accounting in an Early Integrated Industrial: E. I. duPont de Nemours Powder Company, 1903-1912 *

❧ *The appearance of large, integrated industrial firms at the turn of the century encouraged the introduction of innovative accounting practices. Professor Johnson examines the centralized management accounting system that made it possible for one such firm, the DuPont Powder Co., to plan its long-term development and to avoid the internal inefficiency that sometimes accompanies enormous size.*

14

During the merger wave of 1897–1903, large integrated industrials appeared in great numbers for the first time. Although these complex organizations required sophisticated management accounting systems, so far no study has carefully examined the accounting practices introduced by integrated industrial firms.[1] In his description of the emergence of big business, however, Alfred D. Chandler, Jr. stresses the importance of such accounting procedures.[2] Chandler explains that when organizations began to shift from specializing in a single economic activity such as marketing, manufacturing, transportation, or finance, to consolidating two or more economic activities, then "the impersonal forces of supply and

Business History Review, Vol. XLIX, No. 2 (Summer, 1975). Copyright © The President and Fellows of Harvard College.

* The research for this article was supported by grants from two agencies: Canada Council (S70–1226) and Eleutherian Mills-Hagley Foundation (1971 Grant-in-Aid); their generous assistance is gratefully acknowledged. I also wish to thank the following persons for their helpful comments and assistance: Alfred D. Chandler, Jr., the Harvard Graduate School of Business Administration; James Hart and Henry Bryan, DuPont Hall of Records; Richmond D. Williams and his staff, Eleutherian Mills Historical Library; Elaine Bowe Johnson, Huron College; and Richard H. Keehn, the University of Wisconsin, Parkside. The author assumes, of course, the usual credit for errors, omissions, and inconsistencies in the article.

[1] The phrase "management accounting" is used here to mean the "use of accounting information by management" for purposes such as planning and control. Accounting tools that assist management "have, in a significant way, made possible the creation and efficient operation of large enterprises, and it is scarcely conceivable that any business, except the smallest ones, could operate without them." Robert N. Anthony, *Management Accounting: Text and Cases* (Homewood, Illinois, 1964), 359, 10.

[2] Alfred D. Chandler, Jr., "The United States: Evolution of Enterprise" (unpublished ms., September 30, 1970), 71–83; "Recent Developments in American Business Administration and Their Conceptualization," co-author Fritz Redlich, *Business History Review*, XXXV (Spring, 1961), 1–31; *Strategy and Structure* (Garden City, N.Y., 1966), 174–185.

demand" no longer governed "the coordination of the flow of goods from the original producer to the final consumer as well as the setting of prices charged."[3] On the contrary, those firms combining two or more separate activities endeavored to cut costs and raise profits by conducting internally certain transactions that had been mediated in the past by market exchange.[4] Understandably, these new and complex enterprises necessitated the introduction of new organizational structures to control and coordinate their multifaceted activities. One such innovation was the unitary form of organization, comprised of independent departments and one central office to manage both the departments and the entire firm.[5] Although the cost of integrating and coordinating internal activities could limit the size of such organizations and thereby preclude the existence of modern giant enterprise, internal accounting information enables management to monitor and control these administrative costs. Indeed, it is inconceivable that large integrated industrial firms could exist without complex management accounting systems to facilitate assessment, operations, and planning.

15

The records of the E. I. duPont de Nemours Powder Company, an integrated explosives firm founded in 1903, provide an excellent example of the early use of accounting data for management control in an integrated industrial.[6] In order to assess the firm's accounting practices, it is important to recognize that the DuPont Powder Company supplanted the operations of E. I. duPont de Nemours and Company, an explosives manufacturer in America since 1804.[7] The DuPont Powder Company was founded in 1903 by three DuPont cousins, Alfred, Coleman, and Pierre, who, as a result of working during the 1890s for firms that gave impetus to the emergence of modern management techniques, were certain that advanced administrative methods could be applied profitably to the old family firm. The cousins therefore purchased the assets of E. I. duPont de Nemours and Company in exchange for bonds in their newly created firm, the E. I. duPont de Nemours Powder Company. By this trans-

[3] Chandler, "The United States," 56.
[4] This rationale for the integrated firm is an extension of Ronald Coase's transaction cost theory of the firm. See Oliver E. Williamson, *Corporate Control and Business Behavior: An Inquiry Into the Effects of Organization Form on Enterprise Behavior* (Englewood Cliffs, N.J., 1970), 15–18. For other useful insights on vertical integration see George J. Stigler, "The Division of Labor is Limited by the Extent of the Market," *The Journal of Political Economy*, LIX (June, 1951), 185–193.
[5] Chandler, *Strategy and Structure*, 43–50.
[6] The records of the Powder Company are housed in the DuPont Corporation's Hall of Records in Wilmington, Delaware; I examined the records to 1912. References to these records are cited hereafter as "Hall of Records" with the appropriate box or shelf number.
[7] The material in this paragraph is drawn from the superb account of the Powder Company's early history in Alfred D. Chandler, Jr. and Stephen Salsbury, *Pierre S. duPont and the Making of the Modern Corporation* (New York, 1971), 47–120.

action, the owners of the old company gave up their properties in return for bonds, the interest on which was equal to the expected earnings of the old firm. The cousins thus gained control of these properties and became owners of a new company whose stock, which they held, would acquire value only if they could earn more than the previous owners had earned.

In order to raise the efficiency and earnings of their newly acquired company, the DuPont cousins immediately began to develop a new administrative structure to manage their complex enterprise.[8] This structure, which departed radically from the structure of the old family firm, exercised considerable impact not merely upon the Powder Company, but also upon the organization of the entire explosives industry. Before 1903, this industry comprised several independently managed firms, each of which engaged primarily in manufacturing. The old DuPont Company and other major firms in the industry coordinated prices and set output quotas through the Gun Powder Trade Association, a loosely structured, decentralized black blasting powder cartel. After 1903, the cousins rescinded almost all trade agreements in the Gun Powder Trade Association, bought out numerous firms in which DuPont had partial or controlling interest, and consolidated their operations into one centralized, departmentalized enterprise. In short, the DuPont Powder Company became a centrally managed enterprise coordinating through its own departments most of the manufacturing and selling activities formerly mediated through the market by scores of specialized firms.

A centralized accounting system was indispensable to the DuPont Powder Company's elaborate departmental structure.[9] The home office required from the company's mills and branch sales offices, located throughout the United States, daily and weekly data on sales, payroll, and manufacturing costs. These data were then recorded in the basic books of account. From these books the home office accounting department compiled information needed by management to rationalize operations and to increase efficiency. The following analysis indicates that the information provided by this centralized accounting system served two basic purposes. It assisted top management (the Executive Committee) in planning the com-

---

[8] *Ibid.*, 77–120.

[9] *Ibid.*, 144–147. A concise description of all facets of the Powder Company's centralized accounting system is in both R. H. Dunham, "Object of Accounting," a paper for The High Explosives Operating Department Superintendents' Meeting, No. 33 (New York, April 20–26, 1911), and William G. Ramsay, "Construction Appropriations," a paper for The H.E.O.D. Superintendents' Meeting, No. 32 (New York, April 12–16, 1910). These papers are on file at the Eleutherian Mills Historical Library, Greenville, Delaware.

pany's development. It also made possible control and assessment of the horizontal flow of operations within and among the company's three main departments (manufacturing, sales, and purchasing).

ACCOUNTING METHODS FOR LONG-TERM PLANNING

Information provided by the Powder Company's centralized accounting system enabled top management to carry out two basic activities that comprised the task of planning: the allocation of new investment among competing economic activities (including the maintenance of working capital) and the financing of new capital requirements.[10] The first of these two activities, allocation, was relatively unknown to managers of nineteenth-century specialized firms. Allocation became one of the chief occupations of top management, however, in the new integrated industrial firms after the turn of the century. Governing the Powder Company's decisions to allocate investment funds was the principle that there "be no expenditures for additions to the earning equipment if the same amount of money could be applied to some better purpose in another branch of the company's business."[11] The criterion that they used to evaluate any investment project was return on investment.

In making allocation decisions, return on investment was used primarily to evaluate alternative proposals for building new (or improved) manufacturing facilities. Return on investment criteria usually provided a basis for investment decisions only in manufacturing, for in most cases other operations within the company could not be measured directly in terms of profit and loss. One exception, which is discussed below, was the purchasing department's use of return on investment criteria to solve certain investment allocation problems. Most of the company's new investment, however, was in manufacturing. In that area, return on investment data helped accomplish the major task of management planning, namely, the allocation of funds among competing product lines. The Powder Company's accounting system provided information on both net earnings and total investment for each product line and each powder mill. Management could thus allocate capital to new capacity in those products and/or mills that earned the highest return.

The Powder Company may have been one of the first industrial enterprises to use return on investment in management accounting.[12]

---

[10] Chandler and Salsbury, *Pierre S. duPont*, 158–168, 201–217.
[11] Ramsay, "Construction," 2.
[12] The basic figure used by the company for return on investment was net earnings (minus depreciation and before deduction of interest on long-term debt) divided by net

Although business firms used net earnings to measure performance long before 1900, they assessed these earnings, if at all, in relation to costs of operations and not in relation to the firm's total investment in assets.[13] The typical nineteenth-century entrepreneur had little reason, however, to measure return on investment. His chief concern was to control costs and raise efficiency in an operation engaged primarily in one economic activity. Consequently, he took his firm's investment (i.e., the scale of operations) for granted and concentrated on managing short-run costs. The most sophisticated management accounting systems in these early specialized establishments were the cost accounting systems designed by industrial engineers in the steel, traction, and chemical industries.[14]

While the Powder Company's executives recognized that cost control systems were obviously essential to control and assess day-to-day operations, they required more information for long-term planning than that provided by cost accounting systems alone. Whereas most industrialists before 1900 were content to focus on short-run price/cost relationships, the founders of the DuPont Powder Company perceived that "a commodity requiring an inexpensive plant might, when sold only ten percent above its cost, show a higher rate of return on the investment than another commodity sold at double its cost, but manufactured in an expensive plant." They concluded, therefore, that "the true test of whether the profit is too great or too small is the rate of return on the money invested in the business and not the percent of profit on the cost." [15]

An asset accounting system, representing a significant departure from orthodox accounting practice,[16] was the main innovation that

assets (total assets minus goodwill and other intangibles, current liabilities, and reserves for depreciation). For example, see Hall of Records, shelf area 182701-182712, item 107.

[13] Sidney Pollard, *The Genesis of Modern Management: A Study of the Industrial Revolution in Great Britain* (Cambridge, Massachusetts, 1965), 233-245. H. Thomas Johnson, "Early Cost Accounting for Internal Management Control: Lyman Mills in the 1850's," *The Business History Review*, XLVI (Winter, 1972), 474. Andrew Carnegie's company records would seem to demonstrate this early and common practice. Although Carnegie himself assiduously studied operating costs, apparently his company's records did not tie product costs into net earnings, nor did he relate costs and earnings to total investment. One surmises this from the details provided about the Carnegie Steel Company's records (especially William P. Shinn's cost statements) in J. H. Bridge, *The Inside History of the Carnegie Steel Company* (New York, 1903), 84-85, 94-95 and Joseph F. Wall, *Andrew Carnegie* (New York, 1970), 326, 337, 342.

[14] Joseph A. Litterer, "Systematic Management: Design for Organizational Recoupling in American Manufacturing Firms," in James P. Baughman, ed., *The History of American Management: Selections from the Business History Review* (Englewood Cliffs, N.J., 1969), 63-66. Chandler, "The United States," 45-54. Johnson, "Early Cost Accounting," 466-467.

[15] Dunham, "Object of Accounting," 17.

[16] Detailed records of investment in plant and equipment rarely existed in businesses before 1900. Indeed, conservative accounting practice favored charging-off capital expenditures to retained earnings as quickly as possible. Johnson, "Early Cost Accounting," 474. A. C. Littleton suggests that "the nature of depreciation was not yet sufficiently understood to bring forth the suggestion that all expenditures for long-lived assets be charged to asset accounts." *Evolution of Accounting to 1900* (New York, 1933), 236, 245. For an alter-

permitted using return on investment as a tool of management accounting. This system of accounting for the company's productive assets was inaugurated in 1903 when the company made a complete inventory of all its plants and equipment and recorded the values of each item in the general ledger account, "Permanent Investment." Thereafter, all new construction was charged (and dismantled assets were credited) to "Permanent Investment" at cost. The relevant accounting data on construction and/or dismantling costs were supplied through a comprehensive construction appropriation procedure.[17]

The construction appropriation system, in addition to supplying timely and accurate information on total investment, also provided information useful to top management in planning new long-term financing, the second of the two planning activities mentioned above. Since spending on new plant and equipment was the major factor determining the company's need for new financing, information on appropriations and expenditures for construction was imperative for planning new long-term capital requirements. The construction appropriation system supplied, however, only part of the information needed to plan financing. The Powder Company's basic policy was to finance expansion out of retained earnings and the proceeds of stock sales (debt financing was eschewed).[18] Therefore, a forecast of net earnings was required to determine the maximum amount of new construction to which the firm could commit itself.[19] Net earnings were forecast by multiplying the projected quantity of explosives to be sold each month (based on sales department estimates) by the estimated net profit per unit for each product (based on accounting department records).[20] The resulting figure, projected net earnings on sales, was then added to projected non-operating income (e.g., income from land sales, earnings on financial investments, etc.) to get a figure for estimated

19

---

native, but not conflicting, view see Richard P. Brief, "Nineteenth Century Accounting Error," *Journal of Accounting Research*, Vol. 3 (Spring, 1965), 12–31.

[17] In accordance with this procedure, all proposed investment in plant and equipment was described on standard appropriation forms calling for estimates of expenditure, estimates of the savings in cost or other benefits anticipated from the proposed investment, and evidence of proper authorization. Once an appropriation was approved, a report was presented on the final actual expenditure on the new asset. Proper authorities were then expected to account for any unreasonable variance from the original estimate. Ramsay, "Construction Appropriation," *passim.*

[18] Chandler and Salsbury, *Pierre S. duPont*, 210–213, 251–254.

[19] *Ibid.*, 251–252.

[20] Examples of these estimates of net earnings (beginning in October, 1910) are in Hall of Records, shelf area 182701–182712, items 161 and 161A through 161D. Company correspondence in these files indicates that the estimates of profit per unit of output took into consideration probable future trends in both product prices and input costs. Evidence that the company prepared forecasts of net earnings as early as 1907 is in Hall of Records, boxes 184736–184740, item 43.

total net earnings. When combined with data on construction appropriations, moreover, this information on net earnings enabled top management to forecast the company's cash position and thus the anticipated need for new financing.[21] By 1910, the Executive Committee was receiving monthly forecasts of the firm's cash position for a year ahead; both these cash projections and the net earnings forecasts were reconciled regularly with actual results.[22]

Accounting Methods for Short-Term Operations

The second purpose served by information from the Powder Company's centralized accounting system was to enable the vice president of each of the company's three main departments (manufacturing, selling, and purchasing) and his subordinates to control, assess, and coordinate the horizontal flow of line operations in the company. During the last half of the nineteenth century, provision of information needed to control and assess line operations was the main object, of course, of accounting systems employed by specialized firms connected with railroad, metal-working, chemical, electrical equipment, and steel industries. The founders of the Powder Company (and of most integrated enterprises created after the 1890s) had only to refine these accounting systems in ways that would provide data indispensable to coordination of the flow of products between the firm's various internal departments.

A notable consequence of these accounting refinements in firms such as the DuPont Powder Company was that top management (the Executive Committee in the case of the Powder Company) was relieved of most of the burden of administering daily operations that had occupied management before 1900. Top management was able to delegate much of the responsibility for operations to departmental supervisors because of the flow of standardized and reliable information on operating performance and the use of routine operating criteria and instructions. Clearly, then, the sophistication and availability of accounting information increased the Executive Committee's span of control, preventing the loss of control that otherwise might have accompanied the Powder Company's growth after 1903. All conclusions about the company's management accounting procedures may be better assessed, however, after the

20

---

[21] Chandler and Salsbury, *Pierre S. duPont*, 251–252.
[22] Examples of these monthly cash forecasts (beginning in July, 1910) are in Hall of Records, shelf area 182701–182712, item 173. Reconciliations of cash forecasts to actual receipts and disbursements are at item 186. Reconciliations of net earnings forecasts to actual earnings are at Hall of Records, boxes 184736–184740, item 43.

accounting systems used in each of the firm's three main departments are described.

1. *Manufacturing*

Comprising three separate sub-departments (high explosives, smokeless gunpowder, and black blasting powder), manufacturing was the largest and most complex of the DuPont Powder Company's operations. Accounting information permitted control and assessment of manufacturing activities in the company's more than forty geographically dispersed mills.[23] The manufacturing accounting system produced this information in two sets of monthly reports, data for which came in part from mill production control records (such as daily time sheets and daily material usage logs), which the home office audit staff scrutinized periodically.[24] Both sets of reports were distributed to the Executive Committee (on which sat the vice presidents of each manufacturing department), while only one set went to the mill superintendents. The set of reports forwarded to the mill superintendents pertained only to the efficiency of mill production processes; they showed the material and labor used in every stage of production in each of the company's mills.[25] In short, these monthly operating reports contained only information pertinent to the mill superintendents' chief area of responsibility: the operating efficiency of production processes. The reports described both the quantities of raw materials and the dollar costs of all other inputs (except administrative overhead) used by each mill in every production process. These processes varied, of course, among the different mills. For example, high explosives mills made and mixed acids, made nitroglycerine, treated wood pulp, and packed dynamite. For each of these processes, the operating report of a high explosives superintendent would show the dollar costs of non-material inputs and the quantities of raw materials. Use of raw materials was compared both with predetermined standards and with consumption in other mills. The costs in each process affecting non-material inputs were broken down into labor, power, fuel, and

21

[23] Each mill produced only one type of explosive (i.e., smokeless gunpowder, high explosives, or black blasting powder), usually in several varieties, and it also produced many of the intermediate materials (e.g., acids) that were used to make the final products.

[24] The company's only complete cost accounting records, including the accounts for most materials purchased and all payrolls, were maintained by the home office accounting department. The mills kept only those records needed to ascertain the quantities of inputs (material and labor) and the quantities of output for each of their processes. Dunham, "Object of Accounting," 7–13.

[25] Examples of these reports are in the Minutes of the High Explosives Operating Department Superintendents' Meetings on file at the Eleutherian Mills Historical Library. Worksheets for some mill superintendents' reports are in the Hall of Records, e.g., boxes 184736–184740, item 52, "Statement of Charges to Each B Blasting Powder Mill, Month and Year-to-Date for 1908." Also see items 64 and 72.

supplies. Costs per equivalent finished unit of dynamite were also reported. The information in these reports enabled each superintendent to assess his mill's performance both over time and in relation to the performances of other mills in the same department.

The mill superintendents of each department met regularly with the vice presidents of manufacturing to discuss operations and to account for any differences in plant performance revealed by the mill operating units. Apparently, close scrutiny was given at these meetings both to the reports on unit labor costs in each stage of production and to the reports on raw material consumption. The minutes of meetings of the high explosives department reflect careful analysis of mill operating reports and reveal competitiveness among the mill supervisors.[26]

Although the Executive Committee also received the monthly mill operating reports, it concentrated primarily upon a second set of reports (made available only to members of this committee) that provided information about complete products and mills. For each product and each mill, the financial costs of goods manufactured, net earnings, and return on investment were indicated.[27] This information assisted top management in the execution of its primary responsibility: maximization of overall net earnings and return on investment. The monthly manufacturing accounting information sent to the Executive Committee alone emphasized total product costs and related these product cost data to net earnings and return on investment. Information on total product costs was essential, of course, to calculate net income from operations ("operative income from sales"), the basic income figure that the Powder Company used to measure return on investment. Each month the Executive Committee also received a report on operative income from sales, showing for each product the total and per unit amounts for: gross sales, freight expense, selling expense, mill cost, net operative income, administrative expense, and net income. These data were also aggregated by mill and for the enterprise as a whole.[28] The figure for "mill cost" (i.e., cost of goods manufactured) in this report enabled management to analyze both the cost of each product and the manufacturing costs of each mill in relation to overall net earnings. Mill cost was analyzed, furthermore, in great detail in a monthly report that showed its components (ingredients, labor, mill

[26] Minutes of the High Explosives Operating Department Superintendents' Meetings, Eleutherian Mills Historical Library.
[27] Chandler and Salsbury, *Pierre S. duPont*, 146–147. Although a set of these reports no longer exists, many of the worksheets from which the reports were prepared are in Hall of Records, box 133859.
[28] Hall of Records, box 133859.

repairs, power, supplies, depreciation, and work accident insurance)
in total and per unit of output both for each mill and for each of
the company's sixteen products.[29] This information on mill cost
provided the Executive Committee with a perspective on manufacturing costs unencumbered by details on mill operations, yet clearly
related to overall net earnings and return on investment.

In order to appreciate the uniqueness of the Powder Company's
two different sets of manufacturing accounting reports, one should
be familiar with management accounting systems employed in
manufacturing firms before 1903, particularly with the production
control and cost accounting systems that evidently influenced the
design of the Powder Company's mill operating reports. The emphasis on labor and material efficiency in the mill operating reports
of the DuPont Powder Company was also characteristic of the most
advanced manufacturing control systems of the day, those systems
used in the traction, steel, metal-working, and chemical industries.
Many of these early manufacturing control systems were designed
by industrial engineers who had themselves been influenced by railroad accounting practices. One particularly influential industrial
engineer active during the 1890s was Frederick W. Taylor, the chief
exponent of "scientific management."[30] Taylor believed that good
cost records and production control systems were indispensable to
a proper factory management system.[31] Consequently, he concentrated upon devising systems intended to improve management
control over complex, specialized, labor-intensive production processes in the shop and factory. Working for companies in Pennsyl-

[29] The company followed a consistent procedure to account for depreciation. The
balance sheet contained two reserve accounts to cover the cost of replacing obsolete or
destroyed plant and equipment. One, the works accident reserve, covered the cost of
property destroyed in fire and explosions. This reserve was charged 2 cents per keg for
powder and 1 cent per pound for dynamite on every unit of explosive that was manufactured
(Hall of Records, box 133859). The other reserve account, the depreciation account, was
described as "obsolescence insurance, as it [covered] the replacement or rearrangement of
plants or parts of plants, because out of date, or badly laid out according to more recent
ideas, or illogically located on account of change in trade conditions, or, in fact, almost any
reason other than that the plant is worn out or damaged by accident." (Dunham, "Object
of Accounting," 17). The monthly depreciation rates were .5 per cent for plant and 1.25
per cent for furniture and fixtures. Current operating expense was regularly charged, therefore, for all repairs and maintenance to permanent plant and equipment, for the estimated
amount of depreciation due to technical obsolescence, and for the estimated loss that
would arise from fire and explosions. Plant that became inoperative simply because of age
was written-off against operations in the year it was dismantled. Such write-offs were rare,
however, because of the company's maintenance policy and because the company's aggres-
sive policy of cutting costs through modernization caused most facilities to be dismantled,
to accommodate technical improvements, long before they wore out.
[30] Taylor was tutored in accounting in 1893 by Wm. D. Basley, a public accountant
who had many years of experience with railroad accounting. In 1898, when Taylor was
hired to install a cost system at Bethlehem Steel, he stated his belief that the best general
system of bookkeeping is "the modern railroad system of accounting adopted and modified
to suit the manufacturing business," Frank B. Copley, *Frederick W. Taylor*, 2 vols. (New
York, 1923), I, 369–392 and II, 142.
[31] *Ibid.*, I, 364.

vania and Ohio, for example, Taylor's primary occupation was the design and installation of manufacturing cost accounting systems. These cost systems were designed mainly to monitor labor and material costs; they were not intended to monitor financial costs.[32] In fact, since Taylor believed that management's highest objective was to economize labor and material in the factory, he attended exclusively to production efficiency, ignoring commercial efficiency.[33]

It is significant that Pierre S. duPont, Arthur Moxham, and Russell Dunham, who were in part responsible for setting up the Powder Company's accounting system, worked at various times in firms in Pennsylvania and Ohio for which Frederick Taylor designed manufacturing cost accounting systems.[34] Influenced by Taylor's accounting systems, these men devised systems to achieve production efficiency. They sought, however, to achieve more than that. They wanted an internal reporting system that monitored both net earnings and mill operations. In designing this system, they had no obvious precedent. Few industrial firms before 1900 had periodic reports in which overall net earnings were tied in to net earnings on each product sold, and virtually none had periodic information on return on investment. The clearest precedents for the Powder Company's reports were the monthly and annual reports of the Lorain Street Railway Company, one of the Pennsylvania companies with which Pierre duPont was associated around 1900. The Lorain reports showed both the net earnings of each activity undertaken by the firm (real estate development, trolley-line operation, and power generation) and the return on investment in each activity.[35] Pierre duPont's expressed admiration for the Lorain Company's financial control system suggests that he consciously emulated the

---

[32] *Ibid.*, 423–424, 445–448.

[33] "The planning department of the Taylor System, which dealt chiefly in material efficiency . . . neglected market mechanisms and the choices of those planned for or against." Samuel Haber, *Efficiency and Uplift: Scientific Management in the Progressive Era* (Chicago, 1964), 167. *Ibid.*, 17, 165–166. "To Mr. Taylor and his associates costs, though of course important, are secondary to productive efficiency." C. B. Thompson, *The Theory and Practice of Scientific Management* (New York, 1917), 71.

[34] In 1896, Taylor was hired to develop cost systems for the Steel Motor Company and the Lorain Steel Company, subsidiaries of the Johnson Company of Johnstown, Pa. At that time, T. Coleman duPont and Russell H. Dunham were General Manager and Comptroller, respectively, of Lorain Steel. By 1898, when Taylor went to work at Bethlehem Steel, Dunham had moved on to become comptroller of that corporation. Pierre duPont became President of the Johnson Company's Lorain operations in 1899. Copley, *F. W. Taylor*; I, 445, 448 and II, 142, 144. Chandler and Salsbury, *Pierre S. duPont*, 71.

[35] Eleutherian Mills Historical Library, Longwood Manuscripts, Group 10, Series A, File 26–4, "Annual Report of the Johnson Company, 1899." In this report, the net earnings of Lorain Street Railway are compared with net investment; unlike later return on investment calculations of the Powder Company, however, the Lorain figure shows return on stockholder investment rather than total investment.

Lorain reports as a model when he supervised the design of the Powder Company's accounting and internal reporting system.[36]

Two weaknesses existed in the Powder Company's manufacturing accounting system. One difficulty was that the "mill cost" figures did not permit management to make informed "buy-or-make" decisions. Each of the company's mills manufactured many of the intermediate products, such as acids, that were used to make explosives. An important question, therefore, was whether money could be saved by purchasing these intermediate products from outside firms instead of making them in the Powder Company's mills.[37] The Powder Company's cost figures for intermediate products could not be compared with outside market prices, however, because mill overhead and general administrative charges were allocated only to finished goods and not to intermediate products. This accounting policy caused an understatement of the cost of company-made intermediate products (even though these cost data were adequate to analyze the relative efficiencies of internal plant operations). The chief of the home office accounting department argued that allocating mill overhead and administrative overhead only to finished goods prevented informed decisions to buy-or-make. His criticism was opposed by Hamilton Barksdale, the vice president of the high explosives department, who feared that arbitrary allocation of overhead to intermediate products would vitiate analysis of internal plant efficiency.[38]

A second weakness in the manufacturing accounting system was that full financial information on the cost of goods manufactured was reported only to the Executive Committee. Top management was burdened, therefore, with many operating decisions that should have been delegated to the mill superintendents. Moreover, since mill suprintendents were not given complete financial data on mill operations, they were unable to make many decisions that might raise net earnings. The data that superintendents did receive from the mill operating reports encouraged them to economize only in the use of material and labor, but did not necessarily suggest that they reduce dollar costs of production by such means as modifying plant procedures or substituting purchased inputs for company-made

25

[36] *Ibid.*, File 250, "Arthur James Moxham," letter from Moxham to P. S. duPont (March 20, 1900). Chandler and Salsbury, *Pierre S. duPont*, 32–33.

[37] A related question was whether to buy sources of raw materials (i.e., the issue of vertical integration); this question the purchasing department began to deal with in 1908 using return on investment data. See section 3, below.

[38] Dunham, "Object of Accounting," 10–11 and "Discussion," 1–2. Barksdale's viewpoint on this issue seems to run counter to his argument on a separate occasion that interdepartmental transfers should be priced at market rather than cost. See Chandler and Salsbury, *Pierre S. duPont*, 152–153.

inputs. Therefore, even if overhead had been allocated to intermediate products, the Executive Committee and not the mill superintendent would have continued to be primarily responsible for "buy-or-make" decisions. One might suggest, of course, that the manufacturing vice presidents, who as members of the Executive Committee had access to all the company's accounting data, could have supplied full financial data to the mill superintendents. Because the vice presidents were trained as engineers and chemists, however, their natural inclination was to evaluate mill performance in terms of technical efficiency criteria. The mill superintendents were thus encouraged to do likewise. The ultimate answer to the problem of delegating responsibility for making operating decisions to lower-level management did not emerge until after World War I. The solution involved the creation of a system in which the mills became acknowledged profit centers.[39] Mill superintendents then could make informed attempts to accomplish goals defined by top management's objective of achieving a target return on investment.

2. Selling

As in the case of manufacturing, marketing also presented a number of difficult administrative problems to be solved by the Powder Company's centralized accounting system. In the sales department, the major administrative tasks included coordinating customer orders with mill production schedules, keeping advised of market trends, establishing prices, controlling customer accounts, and coordinating and evaluating the performance of the sales staff.[40] The sales department's enormous responsibility for the company's products, which began when goods were finished in the mills and ended when the goods were sold and delivered to customers, was complicated both by the diversity of the company's products and customers and by the wide geographic dispersion of the company's markets. The sales department managed a large network of branch sales offices scattered across the United States; salaried salesmen working out of these branch offices sold virtually all of the company's products. Most of the branch sales offices (and all of the mills) maintained inventories of finished goods. The sales accounting system employed to monitor this complex marketing operation was perhaps the most fully developed part of the Powder Company's management accounting system.

[39] In fact, it was not until the 1930s that the DuPont Company central accounting office (which by then was accounting for separate product divisions) delegated to the mills the task of accounting for prime material costs.
[40] Chandler and Salsbury, *Pierre S. duPont*, 140–141.

26

Although many periodic reports helped management control the Powder Company's sales activities, the sales accounting records themselves (without management intervention) also provided mechanisms for both control and coordination.[41] The primary sales accounting records originated in the field: sales orders and invoices in the branch sales offices and shipping orders in the mills. Copies of these primary records were sent daily to the home office accounting department, which kept all the ledgers for finished goods inventories, sales, and customer balances. The company maintained centralized control over its cash balances by advising customers to remit payment directly to the Wilmington home office. Centralized control was also maintained over branch office and mill inventories by having the home office audit staff periodically verify these inventories.

The most important report prepared by the home office accounting department from these accounting records was the daily sales sheet, a report of the quantity and dollar amount of every product sold by each branch office. These daily sales reports, which offered the vice president of the sales department and each branch office manager timely information (usually with a time lag no longer than four or five days) on market trends, presented data compiled from each day's invoices.

27

Before it appeared on the sales report, the information contained in the invoices was compiled in an unusually advanced way.[42] It was entered on punch cards and then sorted in the fashion of the card-sorting system first used by the U.S. Bureau of the Census in the early 1900s. This punch card system, because of its exceptional flexibility, permitted the home office accounting department to prepare not only the daily sales sheet, but also the following sales reports: a monthly summary of quantities sold and average unit prices by geographic region, by type of product, and by type of customer; a sales cost sheet comparing, among the branch offices, the net prices received and the selling expenses for each type of product sold; a trial balance of finished goods inventories that was reconciled each month with the general ledger. All these reports provided the vice president and staff of the sales department with the comprehensive information indispensable to the control and coordination of the Powder Company's entire marketing activity.

The sales accounting system contributed not only to centralized control; it also encouraged, unlike the manufacturing accounting

[41] The company's sales accounting records are described in great detail in Dunham, "Object of Accounting," 4–7.
[42] *Ibid.*, 5, 19.

system, maximum decentralization of decision making. Nearly all day-to-day operating decisions in the sales department were decentralized; this decentralization enforced profit incentives among the branch sales managers and their salesmen. The procedure for pricing and the incentive-compensation scheme for salesmen were the particular features of the sales accounting system that augmented both decentralization and lower-echelon profit incentives.

Although pricing had been a major task of top management among firms in the Gun Powder Trade Association before 1903, product pricing in the Powder Company was a routine undertaking that seldom required the attention of top management.[43] A committee of sales department executives, the Sales Board, reviewed minimum prices for each product, usually once a month. The review was intended to insure that prices were high enough for each product line to earn a target return on investment. To facilitate pricing decisions, the home office accounting department prepared monthly estimates of the profit per keg or per pound needed to earn a given return (15 per cent for dynamite and 10 per cent for black powder) for the investment in each type of product. Using data on the investment in plant and equipment by product line provided in the construction accounting records, the home office accounting department calculated the percentage of investment that the sales board designated as the earnings goal (e.g., 10 per cent of the investment in black powder capacity) and divided these expected earnings both by the normal output and the capacity output of the mills. The resulting profit needed per unit of output to earn a desired rate of return was then added to the unit cost of production. The resulting total indicated the required minimum price on the product.

A particularly noteworthy consideration that affected the setting of the minimum price on products was the DuPont Powder Company's attitude toward competitors. Convinced that their size and expertise in the industry would always enable them to produce at a lower cost than their competitors, the executives of the Powder Company were not concerned to eliminate existing competition. On the contrary, they regarded the capacity of smaller, higher cost competitors as a buffer to protect the DuPont mills against the excess capacity that would undoubtedly occur during market recessions were DuPont to sell all of the industry's output.[44] Their cognizance

[43] Chandler and Salsbury, *Pierre S. duPont*, 163, 141, 155–157. The method described in this paragraph, which the company used to determine minimum product prices, is not discussed by Chandler and Salsbury; it is inferred from worksheets and correspondence in Hall of Records, boxes 184736–184740, items 27 (B. Blasting Powder) and 39 (Dynamite).
[44] Chandler and Salsbury, *Pierre S. duPont*, 93, 156.

28

of the value of existing competition partially influenced, then, the Powder Company executives' decision to keep prices just below those of competing firms. Information on competitors' prices was gathered regularly by salesmen and forwarded both to branch sales managers and to the home office.

Once minimum price figures were set, they went to the branch sales managers, who had final responsibility for setting the prices charged to customers. A sales manager was allowed to sell above the minimum price, but not below it. His strategy was to set prices as high as he could without risking the entry of a new firm into the industry.[45] While familiar competition served its purpose, new competition was certainly not sought.

Just as the sales accounting system substantially relieved top management's task of making operating decisions by delegating to branch sales managers responsibility for setting prices for individual customers, so the sales accounting system alleviated the administrative task of controlling and assessing the performance of salesmen by designing an incentive scheme that used routinized financial data.[46] Although salesmen were paid salaries rather than commissions, a move designed to strengthen the company's control over its sales force, their salaries were tied to incentives that encouraged salesmen to increase their productivity with a minimum of management intervention. Accordingly, the home office sales department calculated a "normal" volume and a "base" price (not the minimum price) for each product in every branch office. The branch office sales manager allocated his office's "normal" volume among the salesmen assigned to him. If a salesman's actual monthly sales were

29

[45] The constraints imposed on sales managers' pricing activities are outlined in the letter cited in note 46, below. It is notable that the company used return on investment data to judge whether product prices were too high. In late 1906, for example, the Assistant Treasurer of the Powder Company noticed that black blasting powder produced and sold by the company in the anthracite region of Pennsylvania was earning 22 per cent on investment, whereas the same type of powder produced and sold by the company in the rest of the country was earning about 2 per cent. Since all plants were running at full capacity, he argued that the price of black blasting powder should go up about 5 per cent in all districts outside the anthracite region, whereas the price should go down about 8 per cent in the anthracite district. "Unless this is done the story our Profit and Loss statement tells is that while we are selling powder at lower prices than ever before all over the country with a view to preventing further investment in the business, we are inviting the same competition in the anthracite region by having prices which net us practically four times such income on the capital invested as we net in all other territories." Letter from J. J. Raskob to P. S. duPont (Wilmington, 7/27/06), Hall of Records, boxes 184736–184740, item 29.

[46] In a letter dated 4/2/06, the Director of Sales outlined the Powder Company's system for handling the sales force; the system was designed "to give greater latitude to our men in the field [with] handling the trade, . . . to place upon our men more responsibility for the results obtained, and to provide so that their compensation will be varied as closely as possible in proportion with the results obtained along the lines we desire." A copy of this letter is in *U.S. Circuit Court of Delaware, No. 280 in Equity, United States of America, Petitioner v. E. I. duPont de Nemours and Company, et al., Defendants, Defendants' Exhibits,* I, 351–361.

equal to his "base sales" (the base price times his normal volume), then he received 100 per cent of his basic salary. His salary changed proportionately as his actual sales exceeded his base sales. (It appears, however, that a minimum salary was guaranteed if actual sales were less than base sales.) This procedure encouraged salesmen to weigh both price and volume of their sales. In effect, it encouraged them to maximize total revenue for the Company (and themselves) within the constraints imposed by the firm's pricing policy. This incentive procedure also allowed the sales department to direct salesmen's efforts with minimal intervention. For example, the home office sales department provided a direct incentive to a salesman to push one line harder than another simply by lowering the base price of a certain product.

The sales accounting system offered still another means of reducing the administrative responsibilities of top management. It provided a decentralized check on the performance of branch office managers and induced them to control inventories and costs in their branches.[47] The sales department estimated a "normal" ratio of sales costs to gross sales for each branch office. "Sales costs" included general office expenses plus 5 per cent each of the average accounts receivable and average inventory balances. When the ratio of actual sales costs to gross sales was less than the normal ratio, then 7 1/2 per cent of the savings was added to the branch office manager's salary. The office manager was given an additional 5 per cent of the savings to distribute to his staff at his discretion. The Executive Committee received a monthly sales cost sheet that compared gross sales and sales costs by branch office. By creating incentive and establishing control, the Powder Company's sales accounting system helped guarantee that the sales department's performance would contribute effectively to the organization's ultimate goal of raising net earnings.

In a unitary form, multidepartmental enterprise, it is no mean achievement to make the activities of individual departments serve the company's overall goal. Since no common denominator exists to allow comparison of performance among the departments of an integrated enterprise, it is difficult to insure that personnel in each department are contributing to top management's goal of maximum profits rather than pursuing conflicting subordinate goals.[48] Such conflict could not occur, of course, if each department were a profit center whose performance could be measured in terms of either a

30

[47] *Ibid.*, 355–357.
[48] Williamson, *Corporate Control*, 132.

relative contribution to total company earnings or return on investment. Unfortunately, the problem of commensurability is not always solved so easily in the unitary form organization. It is mitigated, however, by such techniques of budgeting and management accounting as those observed in the Powder Company's sales department.

3. Purchasing

The Powder Company's centralized accounting system helped management to control and assess not only marketing, but also purchasing, another activity not readily measured in terms of net earnings. Because the Powder Company's founders perceived that great savings could be achieved if the buying of raw materials were carried out by one department rather than conducted by various individual mills, the purchasing department's activities were located exclusively in the home office. The purchasing accounting system, which in contrast to those systems used by the manufacturing and sales departments did not provide for coordinating and appraising the performance of line operatives, was designed to control expenditure on raw materials, to assess alternative sources of supply, and to coordinate purchasing with production.

The purchasing accounting system centralized control over the ordering, receiving, and expensing of all raw material purchases by relying upon the well-known accounts payable voucher system used in the home office accounting department.[49] The voucher register, first used by railroad accountants during the mid-nineteenth century,[50] offers both convenient control over balances due on account and assurance that purchases are charged to the proper accounts in the proper accounting periods. The purchasing department, which initiated all orders for materials with outside suppliers until about 1908 (when the company began to integrate backward into ownership of supply sources), placed all orders on the basis of market price information. The accounts payable division of the home office accounting department entered each order in a voucher register, issued checks for payment, and provided a monthly summary of all expenses for materials. This summary was derived from the voucher register and provided the basis from which ledgers were posted and cost statements were prepared. Each month the audit staff reviewed all voucher entries and payments.

Having centralized control over purchase transactions, the purchasing department next concentrated upon achieving the lowest

---

[49] Dunham, "Object of Accounting," 2–4, 7–13.
[50] Bridge, *Inside History of Carnegie Steel Company*, 84.

possible prices for raw materials. Until 1908, management had purchased most raw materials from outside agents whose terms were easily compared with market prices. Consequently, very little internal accounting information had been necessary. Indeed, one of the few times that internal accounting information was required took place after 1905 when the Powder Company, which had customarily purchased nitrates through American commission merchants, established its own agent in Chile to buy nitrates.[51] The internal reporting required by the venture was minimal. Regular account was kept of the added cost of the Chilean office, shipping services, and working capital; these costs per ton of nitrate were compared regularly with prices charged by outside agents such as W. R. Grace and Co.[52]

After 1907, the purchasing department needed far more complex management information than had been essential in the past. The crucial reason for this new demand was the national recession of 1907. In their careful assessment of the effects of the recession upon the policies of the Powder Company, Alfred Chandler and Stephen Salsbury point out that the purchasing department's efforts to buy raw materials at minimum price caused a working capital crisis during 1907.[53] As prices fell during the business cycle downturn, the vice president of purchasing accumulated vast supplies of essential raw materials; the payments required for these purchases fell due, however, just as declining orders for explosives reduced working capital. After narrowly escaping the crisis posed by the company's failure to coordinate purchases with sales trends, management revised its purchasing policy to permit the purchasing department to buy at the lowest possible prices only up to a prescribed stock level, the amount of which varied with each month's sales projections.

Although the maximum stock levels imposed by this new policy reduced the risk of a working capital crisis, they introduced the possibility of supply shortages in the event of an emergency. To reduce its dependence on outside suppliers, therefore, the company, although it never achieved full ownership of supplies of all its basic raw materials, began to acquire ownership of many supply sources.[54] The earliest steps toward vertical integration involved controlling the production of such critical materials as charcoal, blasting caps, and packing crates. Each of these inputs accounted for only a small percentage of total purchases. The Powder Company's major raw

[51] Chandler and Salsbury, *Pierre S. duPont*, 185–186.
[52] Hall of Records, shelf area 182701–182712, item 139.
[53] Chandler and Salsbury, *Pierre S. duPont*, 220–228.
[54] *Ibid.*, 228, 187, 204.

material purchases were for nitrate and glycerine. Of these, they chose to integrate backward only into nitrates production; glycerine was always purchased from outside suppliers.

The basic criterion used by the Powder Company to evaluate these steps toward vertical integration was return on investment. Basically, an investment in outside supply sources was approved only if it was judged likely to earn at least 15 per cent per annum, the return the company normally earned in dynamite-making, its most profitable production activity. The purchasing department used two procedures to estimate return on investment in integrated supply operations.[55] One procedure was observed in cases in which the company proposed to manufacture its own supplies of certain inputs (for example, dynamite packing crates or blasting caps). The estimated return, or "profit," on such a manufacturing process was calculated by deducting the estimated unit cost of production from current market price. This estimated "profit" was then divided by the estimated net investment that would be required to build, or buy, the necessary production facilities. A second procedure was followed in cases in which the company proposed to control, but not to own, the source of supply of an essential raw material. This procedure entailed first estimating the savings that would result from buying direct rather than buying through a commission agent. In order to determine these savings, the estimated unit cost of direct purchases was deducted from the market price charged by outside suppliers. Next the purchasing department arrived at return on investment by dividing these savings by the additional investment in inventories that direct buying would require. Although these two procedures have been criticized because they did not take into consideration the effect of the Powder Company's projected production on market prices, it does appear that in fact the company used conservative estimates of market price in order to make these return on investment calculations.[56] On the whole, therefore, these procedures provided useful guidelines for the allocation of Powder Company resources.

33

Conclusion

Many people in the early 1900s believed that large firms, such as the DuPont Powder Company, either would topple from the weight of internal inefficiency or would abuse their market power and pass

[55] Hall of Records, shelf area 182701–182712, items 116, 137, 138, 139, 145.
[56] Chandler and Salsbury, *Pierre S. duPont*, 245.

the costs of bureaucratic inefficiency on to the consumer. Generally, however, the record of the past seventy years suggests that giant enterprise is capable of efficient and acceptable behavior.[57] This favorable record is due in no small degree to "organizational innovations that have permitted the corporation to limit the degree of control loss and subgoal pursuit that, without innovation, were predictable consequences of large size." [58] The management accounting system pioneered by the DuPont Powder Company is a particularly important example of these innovations. This system lowered the cost of integrating each department's activities; it provided routine data that enforced profit incentives on lower level management and staff; and it provided information that helped top management to achieve maximum overall return on investment.

The DuPont Powder Company's management accounting system reduced many bureaucratic problems endemic to a unitary form organization (i.e., a centrally managed integrated organization having several specialized departments). Although a unitary structure is the natural way to organize diverse activities in a single firm, a firm so organized cannot expand in size indefinitely without losing efficiency. The cost of integrating and coordinating internal activities is the main factor limiting the size of a unitary form organization. This cost increases as a firm grows in size primarily because communication of instructions and information throughout the organization becomes more difficult with larger numbers of people. If one compares internal integrating cost with market transaction cost, one sees that a firm will grow until the marginal cost of integrating further transactions within the firm exceeds the marginal cost of mediating the same transactions through the market.[59] Management accounting systems increase the potential size of firms, therefore, by lowering internal integrating cost. Management accounting systems such as the one developed by DuPont Powder Company are the hallmark of big business and they are one of the most important organizational innovations in the modern corporation.

[57] Chandler, *Strategy and Structure*, 44 and Williamson, *Corporate Control*, 4.
[58] Williamson, *Corporate Control*, viii.
[59] *Ibid.*, 14-31. Except for my references to management accounting systems, the comments in this paragraph about limitations to firm size are drawn entirely from Williamson's penetrating analysis.

Management Accounting in an Early Multidivisional Organization: General Motors in the 1920s

By H. Thomas Johnson

Reprinted from
THE BUSINESS HISTORY REVIEW
Volume LII Number 4   Winter 1978

By H. Thomas Johnson

ASSOCIATE PROFESSOR OF BUSINESS ADMINISTRATION
WASHINGTON STATE UNIVERSITY

Management Accounting in an Early Multidivisional Organization: General Motors in the 1920s*

❡ *Introduction of the multidivisional enterprise, which has generally replaced the functional or departmental form of organization in the twentieth century, required management accounting techniques that provided both divisional and top management with data with which to evaluate individual managers' performance, company-wide performance, and future company policy. Professor Johnson discusses the development of these controls at General Motors, the results obtained with them in practice, and their alleged shortcomings, especially in respect to division managers' attitudes towards constructive decisions that might tend to limit in the short run the rate of return on the investment entrusted to them. He concludes with some observations on the influence that organization has had on corporate goals.*

36

The multidivisional organization has been heralded by one economist as "American capitalism's most important single innovation of the 20th century." Because of their multidivisional structure, large diversified companies are able to operate effectively today, whereas sixty years ago their efficient management would have been inconceivable. In his definitive studies of the historical development of multidivisional enterprise, Alfred D. Chandler, Jr. identifies not only decentralized structure but also sophisticated management accounting systems as essential to the multidivisional organization.[1]

Business History Review, Vol. LII, No. 4 (Winter, 1978). Copyright © The President and Fellows of Harvard College.

° The research for this study was supported by funds from The Canada Council and The Eleutherian Mills-Hagley Foundation. The author is responsible for the views expressed in this article. He gratefully acknowledges the assistance of Elaine Bowe Johnson.

[1] Oliver E. Williamson, *Corporate Control and Business Behavior: An Inquiry Into the Effects of Organization Form on Enterprise Behavior* (Englewood Cliffs, N.J., 1970), 175. Alfred D. Chandler's classic thesis on the development of modern large-scale enterprise, including the multidivisional form of organization, is developed in *Strategy and Structure: Chapters in the History of the Industrial Enterprise* (Cambridge, Mass., 1962 and Garden City, N.Y., 1966). His study of multidivisional enterprise and of General Motors in particular is carried further in *Giant Enterprise: Ford, General Motors and the Automobile Industry* (New York, 1964) and *Pierre S. Du Pont and the Making of the Modern Corporation*, co-author Stephen Salsbury (New York, 1971). Additional observations on the importance of accounting information in multidivisional enterprise are found in Chandler

According to Chandler, when companies such as Du Pont, Sears Roebuck, and General Motors diversified after World War I, they discovered that their traditional centralized structures did not suffice for the management of diverse product lines or sales areas. The traditional structure of a centralized company necessitated that top management itself coordinate all of the firm's operating functions, such as selling, manufacturing, transportation, and financing. Necessarily, then, diversification by centralized companies entailed burdening top management with a voluminous and complex flow of internal communications; overwhelmed by the inordinate demands made upon it, top management could neither manage the firm's daily operating activities nor plan its long-run policies.

Eventually giant diversified companies learned that decentralization of management and intricately designed accounting systems would assure the efficient operation of their organizations. A decentralized structure was achieved first by isolating into semi-autonomous divisions the activities of each product or of each sales region. The operations of each division were then placed under the jurisdiction of a general manager. The general manager became responsible for coordinating and controlling all operating activities for one product line or sales region. The only restraints on his authority were the policies and plans established by top management for the company as a whole. Top management, relieved of responsibility for coordinating or monitoring the company's daily operating activities, could concentrate exclusively on planning company-wide policy and assuring that the performance of each division conformed to such policy. While decentralization enabled management to concentrate upon formulating policies and assessing performance, top management's effectiveness depended ultimately upon well-articulated management accounting systems. These systems had to transmit company-wide policy to the divisions and had to convey unbiased information about each division to the central office. Large multidivisional structures, increasingly adopted by today's giant firms, could not function without these accounting information techniques.

An advanced management accounting system was an essential part of the early multidivisional structure introduced at General Motors by William Durant's successors. A brief summary of Durant's own unsatisfactory management procedures will help clarify the importance of the innovative administrative structure designed by

37

and Fritz Redlich, "Recent Developments in American Business and their Conceptualization," *Business History Review*, XXXV (Spring, 1961), 1–31.

Pierre du Pont, Alfred Sloan, Donaldson Brown, and other administrators once they had taken charge of Durant's floundering company in 1920.[2] From its inception in 1912 when Durant founded the company, GM's special distinction was that it consisted of several diversified units, each of which manufactured and sold a unique line of autos or parts. Each unit performed all of the operating functions (such as marketing, manufacturing, and purchasing) that an independent manufacturing company performs; and each unit's administrative system resembled the centralized, functionally departmentalized structures that had been successfully employed by vertically-integrated industrial firms since the early 1900s. Durant's objective in consolidating these autonomous auto and parts manufacturing units into one giant firm had been to achieve financial economies in areas such as manufacturing, finance, and management. He originally envisioned, in other words, a consolidated enterprise whose total profits would exceed the combined profits earned by the constituent units operating as separate companies.

A noteworthy strategy, Durant's practice at GM nevertheless failed, primarily because he was unable to resolve the problems entailed in administering a diversified company. In short, he did not have an administrative system that could direct the activities of each operating unit toward common goals. His unwieldy management procedures, furthermore, immersed Durant in the particular activities of each operating unit. Embroiled in operating details, Durant could not give his attention to general policy-making. Because he could not provide top management direction, Durant prevented GM from achieving the savings that can result from consolidation. Durant's special style of management even prevented many of GM's operating units from performing as efficiently as they might have done as independent companies.

Durant's inability to control GM's diverse operating units precipitated, of course, the well-known inventory crisis of 1920 in which Pierre du Pont replaced Durant as company president. What Durant failed to accomplish, his successors achieved by designing the multidivisional structure in which top management coordinates, appraises, and plans GM's diversified activities without having to supervise its day-to-day operations. GM's well-known multidivisional structure places full responsibility for operating performance on the general

[2] The following remarks about Durant and the 1920 inventory crisis at GM are drawn from: Chandler and Salsbury, *Pierre S. Du Pont*, Chs. 16–18; Ernest Dale, "Contributions to Administration by Alfred P. Sloan, Jr., and GM," *Administrative Science Quarterly* 1 (1956–7), 30–62; Alfred P. Sloan, Jr., *My Years with General Motors* (New York, 1963), Ch. 2.

managers of each division, thereby freeing top management to concentrate on policymaking and to coordinate divisional performance with company policies. This arrangement succeeds because of remarkable innovations in accounting procedures.[3] These procedures allow the multidivisional structure to meld its operating components into a cohesive unit capable of achieving the financial economies contingent upon diversification while preserving the technical advantages inherent in divisional specialization.[4]

Remarkably alert to the importance of management accounting to GM's new structure was a former Du Pont executive, Donaldson Brown. Brown, the chief architect of the accounting procedures introduced at GM, applied to GM the Du Pont Company's advanced and sophisticated financial control techniques. These techniques made possible what GM officials described as "centralized control with decentralized responsibility;" they enabled GM's top management to control the performance of each division without becoming involved in the general manager's administration of his divisional operation.[5]

GM's management accounting system did three things to help top management accomplish "centralized control with decentralized responsibility." First, it provided an annual operating forecast that compared each division's *ex ante* operating goals with top management's financial goals. This forecast made it possible for top management to coordinate each division's expected performance with

---

[3] The sources of information on GM's post-1921 accounting practices that were used to prepare this paper are: Albert Bradley, "Setting Up a Forecasting Program," *Annual Convention Series: No. 41*, American Management Association (New York, 1926), 3–20 (reprinted in Chandler, *Giant Enterprise*, 121–141); Donaldson Brown, "Pricing Policy in Relation to Financial Control," *Management and Administration*, 7 (February, 1924), 195–198 and (March, 1924), 283–286, "Pricing Policy Applied to Financial Control," *Management and Administration*, 7 (April, 1924), 417–422, "Centralized Control with Decentralized Responsibilities," *Annual Convention Series: No. 57*, American Management Association (New York, 1927), 3–24, "Some Reminiscences of an Industrialist" (unpublished mss. at Eleutherian Mills Historical Library, Wilmington, Delaware, 1957); Chandler, *Strategy and Structure*, Ch. 3; Chandler and Salsbury, *Pierre S. Du Pont*, Chs. 17–21; Thomas B. Fordham and Edward H. Tingley, "Control Through Organization and Budgets," *Management and Administration*, 6 (December, 1923), 719–724, 7 (January, 1924), 57–62, (February, 1924), 205–208 and (March, 1924), 291–294; R. C. Mark, "Internal Financial Reporting of General Motors," *Federal Accountant* (November 12, 1952), 31–41; C. S. Mott, "Organizing a Great Industrial," *Management and Administration* 7 (May, 1924), 523–527 (reprinted in Chandler, *Giant Enterprise*, 115–127); Alfred P. Sloan, Jr., *My Years With General Motors* (New York, 1963), Ch. 8; Alfred H. Swayne, "Mobilization of Cash Reserves," *Management and Administration* 7 (January, 1924), 21–23; U.S. Senate, Committee on the Judiciary, Subcommittee on Antitrust and Monopoly, *Administered Prices, Report* and *Hearings*, Vols. 6 and 7 (1958); E. Karl Wennerlund, "Quantity Control of Inventories," *Management and Administration*, 7 (June, 1924), 677–682.

[4] Sloan, *My Years*, 140. Brown, "Some Reminiscences of an Industrialist," 61.

[5] On the development of Du Pont's accounting system to World War I see H. Thomas Johnson, "Management Accounting in an Early Integrated Industrial: E. I. du Pont de Nemours Powder Company, 1903–1912," *Business History Review* XLIX (Summer 1975), 184–204. Brief remarks on changes in Du Pont's accounting system from 1914 to about 1921 are in Chandler, *Strategy and Structure*, 81–82 and 132–133. On the transfer of Du Pont's methods to GM see Sloan, *My Years*, 116–117. Brown, "Centralized Control with Decentralized Responsibilities," *passim*. Sloan, *My Years*, 140.

company-wide financial policy. Second, the management accounting system provided sales reports and flexible budgets that indicated promptly if actual results were deviating from planned results. They specified, furthermore, the adjustments to current operations that division managers should make to achieve their expected performance goals. The sales reports and the advanced flexible budget system provided, then, for control of each division's actual performance. Third, the management accounting system allowed top management to allocate both resources and managerial compensation among divisions on the basis of uniform performance criteria. This simultaneously encouraged a high degree of automatic compliance with company-wide financial goals and greatly increased the division managers' decentralized autonomy.

By promoting coordination with top-level policy, control of divisional activities, and compliance with company-wide policies, GM's management accounting system ensured that top management, without intervening in divisional operating affairs, could guide the divisions' decentralized activities.[6] The following sections describe how this management accounting system facilitated coordination, control, and compliance at GM in the twenties, and in so doing enabled top management to achieve "centralized control with decentralized responsibility."

Coordination of Policy and Operations: The Annual Forecast and Standard Prices

In order to understand GM's basic financial policy, one should be mindful of Donaldson Brown's explicit enunciation of top management's ultimate purpose. Brown said that because "a business owes its existence to its owners" and is therefore "expected to operate for their benefit," top management's central motive is to secure "the permanent welfare of the owners of the business." Brown's professed concern for the owners' permanent welfare may be construed by some, of course, as platitudinous and deceptive. Such sceptics would include, presumably, those who claim that separation of management and ownership in modern large-scale companies seems necessarily to precipitate separation between the goals advocated by owners and those pursued by managers. The legitimacy of Brown's remark, however, is indicated by GM top management's basic financial policy, which places primary emphasis on profit objectives. The basic financial policy that guided GM's top management after 1921

---

[6] Brown, "Pricing Policy in Relation to Financial Control," 195–196 and "Some Reminiscences", 59–65.

was to earn the highest long-run return on investment "consistent with a sound growth of the business."[7] This policy did not mean that the company should strive to earn, in Brown's words, "the highest attainable rate of return on capital, but rather the highest return consistent with attainable volume, care being exercised to assure profit with each increment of volume that will at least equal the economic cost of additional capital required." Top management implemented this general policy in practice by stipulating that the Corporation over the long run should earn average after-tax profits equal to 20 per cent of investment while operating on average at 80 per cent of rated capacity (the so-called "standard volume").[8]

It was extremely difficult, however, to coordinate the company's actual operations in the short run with these long-run rate of return and standard volume goals. The chief reason for this difficulty is that at GM, or any auto maker for that matter, sales and profits in the 1920s fluctuated enormously over seasonal and cyclical trends that were difficult to predict. Contributing to these fluctuations were: the volatile demand for automobiles, a durable capital good whose purchase or replacement consumers could postpone for long periods of time; the practice, industry-wide by the 1920s, by which auto makers announced retail prices at the beginning of a model year and adhered more-or-less rigidly to those prices during the year, even when market demand changed; and the typical auto manufacturer's high fixed costs. Rigid annual prices and high fixed costs meant that an auto maker's profits and return on investment varied greatly, depending upon annual fluctuations in the ratio of output to average annual capacity. These largely unpredictable short-run variations made it very difficult to coordinate short-run operating plans with long-term financial policies.[9]

41

---

[7] Brown, "Centralized Control with Decentralized Responsibilities, 5; Sloan, *My Years*, 141. Other statements that attest to GM management's primary concern with profits are in Fordham and Tingley, "Control Through Organization and Budgets," 719 ("Business is operated only to make a profit") and Mark, "Internal Financial Reporting," 33.

[8] Brown, "Pricing Policy in Relation to Financial Control," 197. Harlow H. Curtice once testified that "standard volume" was based on a daily operating rate of 2 shifts, or 16 hours per day, although he did not state the number of days per year. He said that GM's average production over 30 years (1928 to 1957) was within 7 per cent of "standard volume." See U.S. Senate, *Administered Prices: Hearings* (1958), Vol. 6, 2521 and 2522.

The 20 per cent return on investment rate applied, it would seem, to the Corporation's overall net earnings after taxes. Because corporate expenses *per se* and income taxes were not allocated to divisions, one assumes that the target return on investment for individual divisions, on which product pricing policy was based, must have been considerably higher than 20 per cent. As for what items the company included in its investment base, published accounts give an ambiguous picture. In public statements, investment is often defined as "net worth" or "stock-holders investment" (see testimony by Harlow Curtice cited above). Published examples of the company's internal reports (see Figure 1) suggest, however, that *all* assets were included in the investment base, at least for some purposes. For additional information see Mark, "Internal Financial Reporting," 37–38.

[9] An excellent discussion of the auto industry's interwar pricing policies is in Homer B.

Responding to this difficulty, Donaldson Brown designed a unique annual Price Study that, among other things, enabled GM's top management to coordinate each division's annual operating plan with the company's long-term return on investment and standard volume policies. Each division's manager prepared a Price Study every December for the coming model year (August 1–July 31).[10] Albert Bradley, Donaldson Brown's protégé, has provided a succinct description of the Price Study:

> [The 'Price Study'] embodies the Division's estimates of sales in units and in dollars, costs, profits, capital requirements, and return on investment, both at Standard Volume and at the forecast rate of operations for the new sales year, all on the basis of proposed price. This Price Study, in addition to serving as an annual forecast, also develops the standard price of each product; that is, the price which, with the plant operating at standard volume, would produce the adjudged normal average rate of return on capital which has been referred to as the economic return attainable. Proposed prices can therefore be directly compared with the standard prices which express the Corporation's fundamental policy, and a means is thereby provided for the measurement of departures from the policy . . .[11]

Bradley's statement indicates that a division's Price Study consisted of three basic elements: a forecast at the coming year's expected rate of operations; a forecast at the standard volume rate of operations; and a calculation of each product's standard price. Top management used two of these elements, the forecast at expected volume and the standard price data, to coordinate each division's *ex ante* operating plan with the company's long-run financial policy. These two elements of the Price Study provided, in Bradley's words, "a means of gauging an operating program in terms of the fundamental policy of the Corporation regarding the rate of return on capital investment, as related to the pricing of the product, and the conditions under which additional capital will be provided for expansion." The third element of the Price Study, the forecast at standard volume, provided top management with "a tool for the control of current operations." Before examining the standard volume forecast, detailed analysis of the expected volume forecast and the calculation of standard price are in order.[12]

Forecasting the coming year's expected revenue, costs, and return on investment constituted a division manager's initial task in pre-

---

Vanderblue, "Pricing Policies in the Automobile Industry," *Harvard Business Review* XVII (Summer, 1939), 385–401.

[10] Sloan, *My Years*, 129.
[11] Bradley, "Setting Up a Forecasting Program," 7.
[12] *Ibid.*, 3.

paring the annual Price Study. His first procedure in making the operating plan was to estimate the two components of total revenue: proposed price and expected sales volume. Between the two components, price was presumably the least difficult to predict. The company's policy after 1921 was to restrict the products of each division to a distinct price range. Moreover, the coming year's price had to correspond to current year's prices and to competitor's expected prices. With an estimate of the coming year's price, then, the next procedure in making the operating plan was to estimate sales volume. Each division manager had sole responsibility for establishing the number of vehicles the division would sell and for seeing to it that his division's ultimate sales goal was met. Considerable help with making sales estimates was available, however, from top management's advisory staff. In fact, by 1925 the corporate central office assisted the divisions in making their sales forecasts by estimating GM's share of national automobile demand in each division's price range. The central office derived these estimates from data on expected consumer disposable income, sales trends of the past three years, and the expected impact of style, quality, and price on GM's share of each division's market.[13]

After arriving at an estimate of the coming year's total revenue, the division manager's next step in preparing the operating plan was to estimate operating costs, capital requirements, and return on investment. Available evidence suggests that division managers estimated operating costs and capital requirements by relying upon data on past ratios of costs to output and investment to output, tempering these data, of course, with information concerning expected changes in both factor prices and productive efficiency. Presumably it was not a difficult problem to estimate unit variable operating costs. An estimate of fixed costs, however, particularly those relating to plant investment, was probably more difficult to make. The only available indication, found in a published source, of how the company planned its capital expansion, suggests that management geared new investment both to estimated future output and to the company's standard volume policy (i.e., that annual

---

[13] The detailed steps involved in preparing all segments of a divisional budget were described by two executives of Delco-Light Co. See Fordham and Tingley, "Control Through Organization and Budgets." Limiting the sales of each division to a specific price range followed from GM's overall product policy, enunciated in late 1921, to minimize duplication and competition among divisions. See Sloan, My Years, 65. Although the company's basic product policy indicated a need for some top-level coordination of divisional sales plans, no such coordination existed before 1924. However, top management took a more serious interest in divisional sales forecasts after the overoptimism of certain general managers caused a serious overproduction crisis in that year. For more information on this famous episode in GM's history see Sloan, My Years, 129–134 and Chandler and Salsbury, Pierre S. Du Pont, 549–554. Sloan, My Years, 136–137.

output should average 80 per cent of practical annual capacity over the long run). It may be, as several authorities believe, that the company's standard volume policy provided a means of estimating long-run capital requirements.[14] Certainly the forecast did predict the *actual* investment expected during the coming year. With that investment figure, the net profit calculated from the revenue and cost estimates enabled one to forecast the coming year's actual return on investment.

A divisional manager's forecast return on investment and his proposed prices for a coming year did not inevitably, it should be noted, support and contribute to the basic long-run financial policy formulated by top management. For example, at times when the projected operating rate exceeded 80 per cent of capacity, it is conceivable that top management might undermine its own financial policy even were it to accept a divisional return on investment forecast that was above 20 per cent. The proposed price could very well be too low to ensure that an average return of 20 per cent would be earned over subsequent years, when operating rates might often fall below 80 per cent. To avoid unintentional cases in which proposed prices and forecast return on investment rates failed to contribute to the Corporation's long-run goals, top management compared the proposed prices in each division's forecast with the so-called "standard price." "Standard prices," as Bradley said, "express the Corporation's fundamental policies [and they provide a means] for the measurement of departures from the policy. . ."[15]

In practice, the standard price was stated as a ratio, or mark-up rate, on factory production costs per unit at standard volume.[16] The

[14] Bradley, "Setting Up a Forecasting Program," 7–8; Vanderblue, "Pricing Policies," 397 n. 14, U.S. Senate, *Administered Prices: Report,* 106.

[15] Bradley, "Setting up a Forecasting Program," 7.

[16] To derive Brown's standard price ratio (although in a somewhat different fashion than he follows in "Pricing Policy, . . . ," 283–286 and 417–422), assume a division that produces only one product with capital investment (variable and fixed) K that is comprised of two parts: one a function of sales, f(S) (e.g., the ratio of variable cash and receivables to sales), and the other a function of factory production costs, f(C) (e.g., the ratio of variable inventories to cost and fixed plant investment to cost at standard volume). If S is the division's annual dollar sales, C is the factory production costs (variable, semi-variable, and fixed) at standard volume, a is the "turnover" ratio f(S) ÷ S, b is the "turnover" ratio f(C) ÷ C, and r is the division's target return on investment at standard volume, then

$$K = aS + bC \tag{1}$$
$$\text{and} \quad rK = raS + rbC \tag{2}$$

But rK is also the division's total profit at standard volume, P; and by definition

$$P = S - C \tag{3}$$

If the division's commercial and selling expenses (variable, semi-variable and fixed) are not included in C and if they are stated as a ratio to sales, cS, then

$$P = S - C - cS \tag{4}$$

Substituting (2) into (4) and simplifying, we get

$$(1 - ra - c) \, S = (1 + rb)C \tag{5}$$

Dividing through by the standard volume output, T,

$$S/T = \left(\frac{1 + rb}{1 - ra - c} \right) \frac{C}{T} \tag{6}$$

"dollar equivalent" of the standard price ratio (i.e., the standard price ratio multiplied by factory cost per unit at standard volume) was the factory delivered price that a division had to charge for its output at standard volume (e.g., 80 per cent of capacity) in order to earn the standard return on investment (e.g., 20 per cent).[17] Standard price ratios were calculated, as nearly as one may ascertain, from data in the Price Study's standard volume forecast (discussed below); the ratio remained unaltered until a permanent change occurred either in capital turnover rates, factory operating efficiency, or the division's return on investment target. Because the company applied fixed factory production costs to all units produced at the standard volume rate, moreover, unit factory production costs, by which the standard price ratio was multiplied, varied during the model year only if changes occurred in unit variable material or labor costs. Consequently, the dollar equivalent of the standard price ratio (unit factory costs at standard volume multiplied by the standard price ratio) yielded just enough total revenue to: cover all costs and return 20 per cent on investment at standard volume; cover all costs *except* unabsorbed fixed factory cost at operating rates below 80 per cent of capacity; cover all costs including overabsorbed fixed factory cost at operating rates above 80 per cent.

Given GM's high fixed costs, it followed that if the factory-delivered price charged to dealers always equalled the dollar equivalent of the standard price ratio, then total profits woud yield a return on investment in excess of 20 per cent when the operating rate exceeded 80 per cent; conversely, profits would yield a return below 20 per cent when the operating rate was less than 80 per cent. In theory, the company expected that if the dollar equivalent of the standard price ratio were always charged to dealers during any period of years when operating rates averaged 80 per cent, then the high profits earned when the operating rate was above 80 per

Thus C/T is the unit factory cost at standard volume and S/T is the unit standard price that will return r percent on K at standard volume. Those readers who examine Brown's articles should note that he refers to standard price as "base price" and he generally uses the word "normal" where I have used "standard."

I find it surprising that no economist or accountant has ever derived or analyzed Brown's target return on investment price formula. While economists often discuss GM's standard price policy, they never go into specifics and they seldom refer to Brown's 1924 articles. And accounting writers seem to have ignored Brown altogether. In fact, one group of accountants in 1959 published what they thought was an original return on investment pricing formula; however, they merely reinvented the wheel that Donaldson Brown had already discovered some 35 years earlier. See *Return on Capital as a Guide to Managerial Decisions,* N.A.A. Research Report No. 35 (December 1, 1959), 44.

[17] Although this definition of the standard price implies that the division produces only one product, it is easily extended to a multiproduct (or multimodel) situation if one assumes either that costs and investment can be allocated among products or that the mix of products can be pre-determined. Published information does not indicate how GM actually calculates standard prices in practice.

cent and the low profits earned when operating rates fell below 80 per cent would just average out to a long-run 20 per cent on investment. Given its standard price data, top management felt reasonably certain that *if* the actual prices proposed for the coming model year were in line with the dollar equivalent of the standard price ratio, *then* the operating forecast in a division's annual Price Study would conform to the company's long-run policies regarding return on investment and standard volume.[18]

It should be emphasized that GM did not use standard price data to determine the actual prices to be charged during any given model year. Rather, the main purpose of the standard price policy seems to have been to determine the minimum ratio of price to cost sufficient to make the planned operations of a division comply with the Corporation's long-run financial policy. Top management professed the position that the proposed price for any particular year was determined in the competitive marketplace. The divisional manager's main responsibility, then, was to adjust costs and capital turnover ratios as much as possible in order to assure that his return on investment corresponded to long-run objectives. In other words, if the proposed price for any model fell below the dollar equivalent of the standard price ratio, and if the gap between these two prices could not be attributed to short-run competitive pressures, then top management requested a division manager to reduce his proposed operating costs.[19] Were top management to accept for a prolonged time proposed prices that had fallen below prices dictated by the standard price ratio, surely it would be violating its acknowledged obligation to protect the owners' "permanent welfare." Top management would also request changes in a forecast in which proposed price exceeded the dollar equivalent of the standard price ratio; such action is implicit in its commitment to long-run policies.

46

[18] Alfred Sloan remarked once that "an alternative approach to our standard-volume policy would have been to evaluate prices strictly in terms of actual unit costs at actual or anticipated production levels." However, "the use of the actual unit-cost type of evaluation would have been socially and economically unsound," he argued, because of the industry's cyclical demand and the company's high fixed costs. Naturally, "unit costs would drop in times of high volume and increase during periods of low production. Any attempt to raise prices during periods of low volume, even if competition permitted, to recover the higher unit costs could have deflated sales still further, with the result of still lower profits, less employment, and a generally depressive effect on the economy." See Sloan, *My Years*, 147.

[19] Brown, "Pricing Policy Applied to Financial Control," 417–422. Sloan, *My Years*, 146–148. U.S. Senate, *Administered Prices: Hearings*, Vol. 6, 2519–2521. Dan Cordtz, "Car Pricing, . . . ," *Wall Street Journal* (December 10, 1957), reprinted in *Ibid.*, Vol. 7, 3496–3502. Vanderblue, "Pricing Policies," 396–401. Mark, "Internal Financial Reporting," 34. Homer Vanderblue once suggested that cost does not determine auto price; instead, it determines auto quality. Thus, if division managers regarded the coming year's price as more or less given, they probably coordinated proposed price with standard price by postponing, whenever possible, costly quality (or "style") improvements. Vanderblue, "Pricing Policies," 395.

Clearly, the standard price ratio described above provided top management with a compact and powerful means of coordinating a division's forecast operating plan with company-wide financial policy.

After top management had reviewed and approved the annual forecast and the proposed prices of a division, the forecast was then returned to the division manager. He proceeded to recast the annual figures into monthly estimates, using for this purpose indices of seasonal output trends prepared by top management's advisory staff. These monthly forecasts were then submitted to top management for approval. This submission was expected no later than four months before the operating date; by the 25th of each month in other words, the divisional manager had to provide not only for the current month but also for the coming three months, a forecast including data on plant investment, working capital, inventory and purchase commitments, sales, production costs, and earnings. When top management gave final approval to this four-month forecast, it thereby established the divisional manager's authority to make commitments for production labor, purchases, and other acquisitions. Having reviewed the division's forecasts, top management was now assured that, assuming actual operations went according to plan, the division's performance would conform to corporate financial policy. Thereafter, the divisional manager had complete freedom to implement the operating plans in the forecast, and he assumed full responsibility for his division's final performance.

If their management accounting system had consisted only of the *ex ante* forecasts that coordinated the decentralized operations of various divisions with company-wide policy, Durant's successors at GM would not have achieved their astonishing success.[20] Perhaps even more important than the operating forecast were management accounting procedures that permitted top management to evaluate the division's actual performance frequently throughout the year. By enabling such evaluations, these procedures complement the bene-

47

[20] Although GM's Price Study forecast procedure may have been inspired initially by similar forecasting tools that the DuPont Corporation had used for many years before 1920, it is notable that GM's forecasts by 1923 served a very different purpose than DuPont's forecasts had ever served up to that time. DuPont's forecasting procedure was originally designed to control cash, working capital, investment, and financing requirements; and the forecasts that Durant's successors brought to GM from DuPont in 1920-21 were intended primarily to cope with a severe liquidity crisis. By late 1922, however, when Alfred Sloan said that Price Study forecasts first appeared at GM (*My Years*, 129), the liquidity crisis was gone. Now GM faced the durable capital goods producer's endemic problem of how to control revenue and expense during short-run periods of sharp and unpredictable change in market demand; this problem apparently did not affect DuPont's management to the same degree at that time. Thus, GM modified DuPont's forecast procedures to suit a different set of circumstances. Indeed, most of Du Pont's procedures required modification before they could be used at GM; and one surmises that Donaldson Brown directed the major changes. See Sloan, *My Years*, 118.

fits of the forecast. As in the case of the forecast, they strengthened top management's control over GM's decentralized operations while still preserving the freedom of the divisional manager to execute those operations. By using accounting information primarily on sales and pricing, these procedures helped establish, as did the forecast, top management's control over return on investment. These procedures consisted of sales reports and a flexible budget system.

CONTROL OF OPERATING PERFORMANCE:
SALES REPORTS AND FLEXIBLE BUDGETS

A division's actual operating conditions could deviate from the forecast for a given year in two important ways. Either way demanded prompt adjustment if the planned return on investment were to be achieved. In one case, sales to consumers could deviate from the plan that was established in the forecast. In the other case, the division's production could deviate from the forecast. The following discussion explains the management accounting procedures developed by GM during the 1920s to deal with these two eventualities.

1. *The Ten-Day Sales Report.* A severe overproduction crisis at several of the company's divisions in 1924 taught GM's top management that it takes more than accurate sales forecasts (annual or seasonal) to insure smooth coordination of production and sales. This well-known crisis arose simply because the divisions did not compare their monthly production schedules with timely sales and inventory data from dealers themselves. To prevent production from ever again running ahead of actual demand, the company required dealers after 1924 to submit a detailed sales report to their respective division every ten days. The purpose of these ten-day sales reports was to insure "a change in [divisional] production schedules the moment actual experience indicates a change in the trend of retail deliveries to the public."[21] The uses made of these reports by division managers is described by GM's assistant treasurer in a speech addressed to the 1926 convention of the American Management Association:

> Each car division now receives from its dealers every ten days the actual number of cars delivered to consumers, the number of new orders taken, the total orders on hand, and the number of new and used cars on hand. Each ten-day period the actual results are compared with the month's forecast, and each month, as these figures are received, the entire situation is carefully analyzed to see whether the original estimate was too high or

[21] Bradley, "Setting Up a Forecasting Program," 13. Sloan, *My Years*, 138.

too low. If it is decided that the estimate was too high, the production schedule is immediately reduced. If, on the other hand, it is found that the retail demand is greater than had been estimated, the production program is increased, provided the plant capacity permits. In this way the production program is compared month by month, in fact, ten-day period by ten-day period, and the necessary adjustments in the production schedule and in the estimate of the year's volume . . . are made. In other words, instead of attempting to lay down a hard and fast production program a year ahead and to stick to it regardless of the retail demand, the Corporation now follows the policy of keeping production at all times under control and in correct alignment with the indicated annual retail demand, and with the minimum accumulation of finished product in the hands of dealers for seasonal requirements, which the flexibility of production schedules permits.[22]

To assist a division manager in adjusting his production plans, the corporate central office advisory staff prepared seasonal sales indices and minimum/maximum working capital to seasonal sales ratios for each division. Furthermore, GM received monthly new car registration figures from the R. K. Polk Company, which provided up-to-date information on changes in GM's share of the national automobile market in each division's respective price class. The ten-day sales report system greatly reduced the annual gap between the number of cars sold by GM to its dealers and the number sold by dealers to the public. While this gap amounted to about 10 per cent of sales from August 1923 to March 1924, it was kept to about 1 per cent in 1925 and subsequent years.[23]

2. *Flexible Budgets.* Although ten-day sales reports enabled one to detect changes in market demand and thereby to adjust forecast production schedules, further data were needed to evaluate the changes in costs, profits, and return on investment that occurred when the output level became different from the level that was planned in the original forecast. Indeed, if information in the sales reports caused a division manager to change his output level, then the actual profits and return on investment for his division would naturally vary from the planned amounts in the original forecast, given the typical auto maker's high fixed costs and inflexible prices. When such changes occurred, it was important to know if the resulting variance between actual net income and forecast net income was due exclusively to unplanned changes in the level of output, in which case the income variance is purely a function of uncontrollable fixed costs, or if the variance was due to unplanned changes in controllable costs, operating efficiency, or other factors

49

[22] Bradley, "Setting Up a Forecasting Program," 13.
[23] Sloan, *My Years,* 138; Ernest Dale, *The Great Organizers* (New York, 1960), 100.

unrelated to the level of output. In other words, did actual income differ from forecast income because the division's sales volume did not match the planned level, or because the division's operating efficiency was not at planned levels? Modern management accountants use the "flexible budget" to compare forecast results with the results attained at actual levels of output. The flexible budget distinguishes between variable (or controllable) costs and fixed (or uncontrollable) costs, and thereby projects forecast total costs and profits at any level of output (within a given amount of fixed capacity).

Accounting and business historians suggest that flexible budgeting was barely discussed in accounting literature before the 1920s. One authority takes the extreme view that "it was not until the late 1930s that refined techniques for relating cost to size of output in the short-run were developed." Other writers, however, have noted that flexible budgeting systems actually were being used by 1927 at the Gillette Safety Razor Company and by the late 1930s at the Westinghouse Electric Corporation. As early as 1924, however, Donaldson Brown, in a series of three articles on GM's pricing and budgeting procedures, described a refined and ingenious technique for relating cost, net profit, and return on investment to short-run output variations. Nowhere in these articles does Brown refer to his technique as "flexible budgeting;" nevertheless, he does make it clear that his pricing and budgeting procedures were designed primarily so that the large annual and seasonal variations of sales and output that typified GM's operations would not vitiate management's efforts to control costs and profits. His revolutionary procedures, which have been either misunderstood or ignored by historians, gave GM a fully articulated flexible budget at least as early as 1923.[24]

GM's flexible budget was based on the standard volume forecast contained within each division manager's annual Price Study. The standard volume forecast, as I mention above, projected operations for the coming model year at the proposed unit price and the standard volume (i.e., 80 per cent of planned capacity). This forecast at standard volume established "standard" values for all of the major factors, such as fixed cost, variable cost, and capital turnover, that

[24] Robert H. Parker, *Management Accounting: An Historical Perspective* (London, 1969), 67–70; David Solomons, "The Historical Development of Costing," in D. Solomons, ed., *Studies in Costing* (London, 1952), 36; on Gillette see R. H. Raymond, "History of the Flexible Budget," *Management Accounting* (August, 1966), 12; on Westinghouse see Dale, *The Great Organizers*, 151 and 165–166; Brown, "Pricing Policy . . . Financial Control." "In these annual budgets, fixed and non-variable expenses are treated separately from variable so that the figures can be readily adjusted for changes in volume at any time during the year," Sloan, *My Years*, 143. See also Mark, "Internal Financial Reporting," 34.

affect return on investment. Specifically, the forecast showed each of the following items as percentages of total sales (at the proposed price and standard volume): variable costs, fixed costs plus net profit, variable working capital, and fixed investment. These ratios (and ratios of these same items to factory cost at standard volume) were frequently used to project the cost and investment figures in the actual operating plan that a division manager incorporated into his annual forecast.[25] Their main purpose, however, was to provide norms, thus enabling assessment of deviations between the division's forecast and its actual operating performance. By using these standard volume ratios in a simple formula, one could calculate what the annual net return on investment *should* be at *any* volume of output (at the coming year's proposed price and with total plant capacity given) in order to satisfy top management's basic financial objective. These same standard volume ratios also made it possible, assuming appropriate seasonal adjustments for production and fixed cost factors, to predict each *month* what the return on investment should be at any relevant volume.

51

Table 1 illustrates the essential features of GM's standard volume forecast, and it demonstrates how the standard volume ratios were used to project an operating forecast at output levels other than standard volume. The data in the table apply to a hypothetical operating division manufacturing one product that it intends to sell at the standard price. The division's rated annual capacity is 50,000 units per year, or a standard volume of 40,000 units (80 per cent of rated capacity). Factory cost is applied to all units produced at a fixed rate that is based on standard volume. Any over/unabsorbed burden is charged directly to operating income. As Donaldson Brown pointed out, GM did not use standard costs *per se* in the 1920s. Rather, the company costed output at actual prime costs plus a predetermined burden rate (at standard volume). The difference between actual and applied burden was charged directly to income. (Actual commercial expense, however, was charged directly to operating income. Table 1 shows the portion of commercial expense that is fixed; reasons for this are presented below.[26]

As an illustration, Table 1 shows the complete financial information at two output levels other than that of standard volume. In

[25] Fordham and Tingley, "Control Through Organization and Budgets," 722.
[26] To preserve simplicity, the annual sales are forecast in Table 1 using the dollar equivalent of the standard price ratio. In practice, however, division managers prepared the standard volume forecast using the actual price that was proposed for the coming model year (see Bradley, "Setting Up a Forecasting Program," 7); Brown, "Centralized Control with Decentralized Responsibilities," 21, and "Pricing Policy in Relation to Financal Control," 285.

TABLE 1
DIVISIONAL RETURN ON INVESTMENT FORECAST

Item	Standard Volume	Ratio to Sales*	Proposed Volumes Above Standard	Ratio to Sales	Below Standard	Ratio to Sales
Annual sales in units	40,000	—	50,000	—	30,000	—
Proposed price per unit	$ 1,250	—	$ 1,250	—	$ 1,250	—
Profit and loss statement:						
Annual sales	$50,000,000	1.000	$62,500,000	1.000	$37,500,000	1.000
Factory cost of sales —						
Variable portion	35,000,000	.700	43,750,000	.700	26,250,000	.700
Fixed portion applied at $125 per unit	5,000,000	.100	6,250,000	.100	3,750,000	.100
Gross factory profit	10,000,000	.200	12,500,000	.200	7,500,000	.200
Add overabsorbed factory burden	—		1,250,000	.020	—	
Deduct unabsorbed factory burden	—		—		1,250,000	.020
Commercial expense, actual (Fixed portion is $2,300,000)	3,500,000	.070 (.046)	3,800,000	.0608 (.0368)	3,200,000	.0853 (.0613)
Net profit from operations	$ 6,500,000	.130	$ 9,950,000	.1592	$ 3,050,000	.0813
Capital investment statement:						
Working capital	$17,500,000	.350	$21,875,000	.350	$13,125,000	.350
Fixed investment	15,000,000	.300	15,000,000	.240	15,000,000	.400
Total investment	$32,500,000	.650	$36,875,000	.590	$28,125,000	.750
Return on investment, annual percent	20.00		26.98		10.84	

Source: Adapted with minor changes from Table 15 in Donaldson Brown, "Pricing Policy Applied to Financial Control," 421.
Note: * Those standard volume ratios which pertain to the standard price ratio that is described in footnote 16 are: r = .200; c = .700; a = an arbitrarily chosen value, say .150; b = (.650 − a) 50/40 = .625.

order to calculate return on investment at any proposed operating level, one needs to know, however, only the relevant ratios of cost and investment to sales *at standard volume*. To follow Donaldson Brown's procedure for calculating what the standard return on investment dictated by top-level policy *should be* at any proposed operating level, let a = the ratio of fixed factory and commercial costs to sales, let b = the ratio of net profit to sales, let c = the ratio of working capital to sales, and let d = the ratio of fixed investment to sales. Then, if the ratio of the proposed volume to standard volume is m, and if the return on investment at the proposed volume that satisfies top management's long-run policy is x,

$$ x = \frac{b + a\left(\dfrac{m-1}{m}\right)}{c + \dfrac{d}{m}} . $$

In Table 1, the values of the ratios at standard volume are: a = .146; b = .130; c = .350; d = .300. Thus, at an operating level of 50,000 units m is equal to 1.25 and x = 26.98 per cent.

As this equation indicates, the ratios in the standard volume forecast enabled top management and the division manager to compare easily and rapidly the *ex post* return on investment at any operating level (e.g., 50,000 units) with the desired return that was dictated by corporate long-run policy (i.e., 26.98 per cent at 50,000 units). Any discrepancy between the actual rate of return and the desired rate was caused either by unanticipated deviations from the projected selling price, unplanned changes in factor prices, or unexpected alterations in operating efficiency. Unless identified and compensated for, a variation between the actual and desired rates of return could prevent a division, of course, from achieving the long-run financial objective established for it by top management. Records indicate, however, that GM's managers detected such deviations by comparing the actual price, cost, and capital ratios, adjusted for seasonality, to the standard volume ratios. Each division prepared not only monthly, but even *daily* reports designed specifically to compare actual results in every aspect of operations with the standard volume results that had been predicated upon GM's top-level goals for return on investment.[27]

[27] Examples of some of these reports are in Mark, "Internal Financial Reporting," 36. Albert Bradley once noted that "on the basis of our forecast we work up a balance sheet and income statement [and] during each month as it develops we make up a daily balance sheet and income account, so that we can tell you this afternoon where we stood at the close of business yesterday." See the discussion that follows "Setting Up a Forecasting Program," 19.

Perhaps the most important of these operating reports was the division's monthly analysis of return on investment. This analysis, which identified the precise effect that every income and balance sheet item had on final return on investment, employed the variables in the return on investment formula developed by Donaldson Brown at Du Pont in 1915 and introduced at GM after the war. Brown's formula simply states that R (return on investment) = P (ratio of net profit to sales) x T (ratio of sales to capital investment). Return on investment is, in other words, the product of the margin on sales and the rate of capital turnover. For purposes of analysis, one can disaggregate P into as many components as there are entries in a profit and loss statement and T into the number of entries in the balance sheet. In effect, such disaggregation is done in the analysis illustrated in Figure 1. The actual figures in a monthly analysis presumably came from the standard forecast budget and current operating statements.

The format used in Figure 1 constituted a unique management report not because it evaluated operations in terms of return on investment; such analyses were not unusual in the twenties. GM's report was exceptional because it enabled top management to assess whether actual operating results conformed to top-level policy. At a glance, they could compare actual values and the standard values for the latest month's operations. By showing succinctly the effect of a division's operating results on return on investment, the report shown in Figure 1 reinforced top management's centralized control while freeing it from having to consider details pertaining to a division's decentralized operations. The format of the analysis in Figure 1 has the additional advantage of encouraging division managers to consider each operating factor in terms of its ultimate impact on return on investment.[28]

In order to appreciate the ramifications of GM's standard volume ratios, one must consider how division managers used these ratios in Brown's standard price ratio to evaluate current prices. If we put the standard volume ratios from Table 1 into the standard price ratio that is described above in footnote 16, then $r = .200$, $a = .150$, $b = .625$, $c = .070$; and the standard price ratio is $\frac{1.125}{.900}$, or 1.250. The dollar equivalent of the standard price ratio, therefore, is \$1,250 (1.250 times the unit factory production cost at standard volume). As I noted earlier, the standard price ratio (1.250) does not change unless the capital turnover rates or the target return on investment

[28] Brown, "Some Reminiscences of an Industrialist," 48–49.

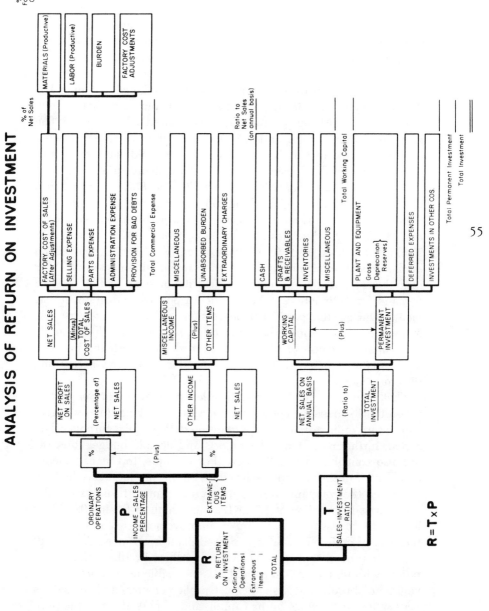

FIGURE 1

Source: Donaldson Brown, "Some Reminiscences of an Industrialist," 129. (Reproduced by permission of Eleutherian Mills Historical Library, Greenville, Delaware.)

EARLY MANAGEMENT ACCOUNTING   509

rate change. The standard price ratio helped one estimate, however, how much actual prices should change in order to compensate for unanticipated changes in variable unit factory costs (i.e., material prices, wages, etc.). By applying the ratio to changes in unit labor or material costs, the division manager determined how much he had to change the stated selling price in order to continue to earn the budgeted return on investment at the budgeted volume. His decision to change price depended finally, of course, on factors such as competitive pricing pressures and anticipated sales results.[29] The standard volume ratios and price formula quickly revealed what effect a change in variable operating costs would have on return on investment if the division manager did *not* change price.

3. *Results of GM's Sales Report and Flexible Budget Procedures.* Countless factors affect the long-run performance of a company. Some of the major variables affecting GM's performance were controlled after 1921 by sales reports and flexible budget systems. As Table 2 indicates, after its reorganization in 1921 GM enjoyed an extraordinary return on investment and remarkable expansion. Year in and year out, despite many radical fluctuations in the national demand for automobiles, GM recorded a positive return on investment. During the post–1929 depression it was one of very few major U.S. corporations that did not register losses. Undoubtedly one important cause of GM's success in dealing with the problem of fluctuating annual demand was Donaldson Brown's accounting system.

That management effectively handled fluctuations in demand as a result of its management accounting system is suggested by aggregate return on investment and expansion data. Capital turnover data reveal, furthermore, that sales reports and flexible budget forecasting also contributed to efficiency. For example, top management's improved forecasting and a levelling-off of production schedules permitted the company to raise its average annual turnover of total inventories from a low of 1.5 in 1921 to a high of 6.3 in 1925. It is legitimate to assume that similar improvements occurred in the turnover of cash, receivables, and fixed plant investment. As a result of this improved turnover, according to Albert Bradley, "the corporation, with no increase in capital, has been able to conduct a larger volume of business at a smaller net profit per unit, and to make a very satisfactory return on its capital; and to pass along to the pub-

[29] "In order to allow for freedom of action with respect to variations in raw material and labor prices, it is not desirable to establish the [standard price] in terms of dollars per unit of product, but rather in terms of percentage of factory cost [at standard volume]." Brown, "Pricing Policy in Relation to Financial Control," 285, 286.

TABLE 2
SELECTER PERFORMANCE INDICATORS,
GENERAL MOTORS CORP., 1920–1929

	Return on Investment (%)[a]	Net Sales ($000,000)	Average Number of Employees (000)	Share of U.S. Automobile Market (%)[b]
				(1919) 21
1920	8.8	567	81	N/A
1921	(10.6)	304	46	13
1922	13.5	464	65	N/A
1923	16.5	698	91	20
1924	11.5	568	74	N/A
1925	23.8	735	83	20
1926	29.4	1,058	130	N/A
1927	31.0	1,270	176	43
1928	32.3	1,460	209	N/A
1929	26.0	1,504	233	32
				(1931) 43
Avg. 1920–29	18.2			
Avg. 1927–55	21.7			

Source: Chandler and Salsbury, *Pierre S. du Pont and the Making of the Modern Corporation* (1971), 612–614. The average for 1927–55 in column 1 and the figures for 1919 and 1931 in column 4 are from *Hearings on Administered Prices: Automobiles* (1958), Part 7, 3862–3.

Notes: [a] Column 1 is net income (after taxes) divided by the sum of capital stock and surplus.
[b] Column 4 represents the percentage of U.S. new car registrations sold by G.M. each year.

lic the savings resulting from increased volume and increases in efficiency." [30]

COMPLIANCE WITH TOP-LEVEL OBJECTIVES

We have seen that particular features of GM's management accounting system helped top management to coordinate and control divisions, clearly establishing financial objectives for their division managers. Other features in the system helped motivate division managers to comply with these company-wide financial goals. These mechanisms for compliance considerably increased the probability that top management's financial goals would in fact be achieved.[31]

[30] Bradley, "Setting Up a Forecasting Program," 15–18.
[31] Accountants have studied the effects of internal accounting systems on management behavior and economists have studied the effects of internal structure on company performance only in the past decade or two. Thus, GM's New Era management system anticipated management accountants' and economists' ideas about motivating profit-oriented behavior by almost fifty years. For some additional insight into how advanced GM's management accunting system was, see Fordham and Tingley, "Control Through Organization and Budgets," 291–294.

Before discussing these accounting mechanisms for compliance, the goals themselves must be considered. Although some modern economists argue that multidivisional structure gives top management unique power to advocate profit-oriented goals, most authorities contend that when top management in any large-scale enterprise sets goals, it is not influenced by profit motives of the sort associated with neoclassical profit maximizing behavior.[32] This proposition is based upon the following argument. It is claimed that in very large firms a gulf invariably separates top management both from the owners of the company and from the competitive pressures of the market. This gulf necessarily weakens top management's commitment to profit objectives. Top management in a large organization, it is argued, will not pursue purely profit-oriented goals unless a highly concentrated and powerful group of owners forces it to do so. Challenging this viewpoint is the contention that a company's organizational structure significantly influences the nature of the goals established by top management. The multidivisional structure, for example, by decentralizing all of a company's operations into profit centers or investment centers, enables top management to judge whether or not a division manager's performance contributes to company-wide profits. It frees top management, in other words, to formulate company-wide goals that are profit-oriented. Noteworthy is the fact that among large companies, those with multidivisional structures are able to advocate entrepreneurial goals, whereas centralized, functionally departmentalized firms are often forced to accept goals that sacrifice company-wide profits.[33]

[32] The unique goal pursuit properties of the multidivisional structure are summarized in Williamson, *Corporate Control*, Ch. 8. (especially 133–134). A succinct statement of economists' views on corporate goal formation is in F. M. Scherer, *Industrial Market Structure and Economic Performance* (Chicago, 1970), 31–33 and 282–283. A more elaborate discussion of economists' theories of corporate goal formation, including a thorough examination of the behavioral theory of the firm, is in Kalman J. Cohen and Richard M. Cyert, *Theory of the Firm: Resource Allocation in a Market Economy* (Englewood Cliffs, N.J., 1965), Chs. 16–17.

[33] Top management's dedication to "entrepreneurial" profit-making is theoretically no less in a centralized company where operating responsibility is delegated to functional department managers than it is in a decentralized company, like GM, where operating responsibility is delegated to division managers. In practice, however, it is often quite different. In the functionally departmentalized firm, top management often finds that it must sacrifice some of its commitment to company-wide profits in order to achieve smooth coordination of the operating departments' activities. The reason is that the performance of these departments, since they are cost centers or revenue centers, cannot easily be evaluated in terms of their contribution to company-wide net profit. Except where a department head's performance is egregiously bad, then, it is difficult to detect, especially in large organizations, if department heads are doing everything they can to enhance company-wide profits. Therefore, top managers in large-scale functionally departmentalized firms often find that the easiest way to achieve smoothly coordinated operations is to trade-off some company-wide net profit for a certain amount of departmental "slack" (e.g., overstaffing, inefficiency, and so forth), to the extent that market conditions allow such a trade-off to be made. See Oliver E. Williamson, "Managerial Discretion, Organization Form, and the Multi-division Hypothesis," in Robin Marris and Adrian Wood, eds., *The Corporate Economy: Growth, Competition, and Innovative Potential* (Cambridge, Mass., 1971), 358–359.

Although the multidivisional structure makes it possible for top management to advocate profit-oriented goals such as those established by GM in the early twenties, it cannot by itself ensure that these objectives will be realized. The company's internal accounting system must also encourage divisional managers to comply with these company-wide goals. Specifically, the accounting system must establish proper criteria to judge divisional financial results. Furthermore, the accounting information about divisional financial results must be accurate and timely. Proper criteria and timely, accurate reporting are both necessary in order to encourage subordinate managers to pursue the same entrepreneurial objectives that top management establishes for the entire company.

Some modern authorities contend that the chief criterion used by top management at GM to evaluate divisional performance results, return on investment, often fails to impel division managers to adopt an entrepreneurial attitude. This failure occurs, they say, because return on investment is sometimes an unreliable indicator of a division's contribution to company-wide profits or of the performance of a division manager. While these limitations obviously impair the usefulness of return on investment, they nevertheless can be circumvented. Safeguards contained within GM's internal accounting system assured that return on investment would serve as a valid criterion.

Should a division manager, for instance, attempt to meet top-level return-on-investment goals by underinvesting, he diminishes company-wide profits. Such underinvesting may be prevented by depriving divisional managers of discretion in planning new investment. As one authority points out, "the rate of return is only a satisfactory measure of the performance of a division in those instances where the divisional management has little or no control over the level of investment in the division."[34] This statement implies, ironically, that GM's divisional return-on-investment data, which helped top management to achieve "decentralized responsibility," should have required total centralization of all investment planning. However, two features of GM's management accounting system not only prevented division managers from bolstering return on investment by underinvesting, but did so without infringing on their discretion to plan investment spending. In the first place, the annual forecast included plans for expansion that division managers worked out only in close collaboration with top management. The role of the

[34] David Solomons, *Divisional Performance: Measurement and Control* (Homewood, Ill., 1965), 154.

corporate staff in assisting with sales and capital turnover estimates minimized divisional bias in these plans. These expansion plans, presumably stated in terms of expected unit sales, surely placed a lower bound on each division manager's planned investment. The annual forecast therefore compelled a division manager to achieve return on investment targets *without* stinting on expansion plans. In the second place, the company's financial reporting system greatly emphasized capital turnover ratios. By frequently reminding division managers about the relationship between capital turnover and return on investment, the management accounting system promoted initiative and ingenuity in raising capital turnover ratios. By implication, this meant that division managers had considerable discretion in planning specific investment projects.

Today analysts call attention to yet another difficulty with return on investment data. They explain that comparisons of divisional return on investment results do not always properly indicate the comparative performance of the division managers themselves. Indeed, a capable manager who takes over a division that already has chronic and deep-rooted troubles might be evaluated unjustly were his return on investment to be compared with that of other divisions rather than with his own division's past or potential performance. Because top management in a multidivisional firm has the power to allocate resources among the firm's operating units, and because a division manager's search for additional resources encourages him to comply with top-level goals, resources must not be allocated strictly according to differential return on investment results. Indeed, in order to maintain company morale, GM's top management as far back as the 1920s apparently assessed divisional managers occasionally in terms of differing targets for return on investment, the target depending upon the division in question.[35]

As nearly as one can tell, GM's return on investment criterion for judging divisional financial results provided proper motivation, then, for division managers to pursue top management's entrepreneurial goals. Further motivation was supplied by the timely and accurate reporting of divisional financial results to GM's top management.

[35] The problem of distinguishing between the division's performance and the division manager's performance is succinctly analyzed in Charles T. Horngren, *Cost Accounting: A Managerial Emphasis* (Englewood Cliffs, N.J., 1977), 713. "To the extent that performance and subsequent resource assignments can be connected in rational ways, the resource allocation process can be made responsive to differential performance. *Ceteris paribus*, those parts of the organization that are realizing superior performance will increase in relative size and importance, with all of the beneficial local gains associated with expansion." Williamson, "Managerial Discretion," 362. Different return-on-investment targets existed for different products at least since 1910 at the DuPont Corporation, whose methods provided so many of the basic ideas for GM's post-1921 accounting system. Johnson, "Management Accounting in an Early Integrated Industrial," 198–199.

The return on investment data sent to top management related each division's performance directly to top-level goals. These data were prepared in all divisions according to company-wide accounting standards; they were audited by top management staff personnel; they were compiled for top management by corporate staff personnel whose company-wide perspective freed them from divisional biases; and they were timely. These data revealed promptly and unambiguously, therefore, any failure of a division manager to meet the company's basic financial objectives. In so doing, they enabled top management to swiftly remove a division manager who failed to perform as expected. Obviously such a reporting system put enormous pressure on the division manager to remove slack and inefficiency at all levels within his division. Acknowledging the intensity of pressure on a division manager to comply with top-level profit goals, one modern economist suggests that a functionally departmentalized division within a multidivisional firm should generally be more profitable than an independent functionally departmentalized firm of similar size.[36]

It would seem, then, that the internal accounting features of the multidivisional structure not only enable top management to espouse profit-oriented goals, but also to prompt entrepreneurial behavior within the divisions themselves. There are countless situations, of course, in which a division manager may reduce the company's overall profits in order to maximize the profits of his particular division. Such "dysfunctional" situations most often arise when a company's decentralized divisions are highly interdependent.[37] When interdependence exists, therefore, it is usually necessary to restrict divisional autonomy.

Although many cases occur involving dysfunctional behavior and requiring varied solutions, buying and selling among divisions deserves our close attention. This activity is undoubtedly the most important one that can be influenced by a management accounting procedure *per se*. This management accounting mechanism, known as transfer pricing, has the effect in some cases of interdivisional trad-

[36] It is notable that division controllers at GM were the only company officials who had dual responsibility; they reported both to the division manager and to the corporate controller. Williamson, *Corporate Control*, Ch. 8. An independent functionally structured firm will tend to be less profitable than a semi-autonomous division of similar size largely because the chief executive of the independent company is under less pressure than the general manager of the division to suppress slack and inefficiency within his organization. Whereas the performance of the division manager is promptly and comprehensively scrutinized by profit-oriented top managers, the performance of the independent company's chief executive is evaluated infrequently and imperfectly by outsiders (e.g., participants in capital or product markets, stockholders, "raiders," and so forth) whose incomplete knowledge about the company's operations precludes them from threatening the chief executive's position unless his performance is egregiously bad.

[37] Horngren, *Cost Accounting*, 742–744.

ing of preventing one division's actions from lowering the profits of other divisions and the entire company. GM has published very little specific information about its actual internal transfer pricing policies. We do know, however, that the company's general policy required selling divisions to charge market prices on items sold to buying divisions.[38] Market transfer pricing will preserve divisional autonomy and minimize the dysfunctional consequences of inter-divisional trading only as long as two conditions exist, of course, in the market for the product involved: the market must be competitive and it must not be affected greatly by the company's own supply and demand. In the absence of these two conditions, "market" transfer pricing may have dysfunctional consequences. Only by using other transfer pricing procedures designed to further limit divisional autonomy can such consequences be avoided. Scanty information about GM's transfer pricing procedures prevents calculating the effect those procedures have had on the company's overall performance since 1921.

All factors, such as dysfunctional activity, that widen the gap between perfect compliance with company-wide objectives and actual compliance cannot, however, be controlled by management accounting techniques alone. For example, in the case mentioned above, GM acknowledged the potentially dysfunctional consequences of competition among every automobile division; consequently each division's autonomy was limited by restricting its sales to unique, non-overlapping price ranges. To reduce similar dysfunctional activities in areas such as research, engineering, purchasing, and advertising, GM established a number of interdivisional committees.[39]

In addition to these procedures for controlling dysfunctional activities, GM used one additional means to achieve compliance: a plan for salaried executives that provided bonus incentives. Bonuses were based on divisional performance records; however, they were given in the form of rights to GM common stock. Moreover, a manager's stock bonus for any given year became vested only if he stayed with GM for an additional period of time, usually five years. Therefore, the value of the bonus to an executive depended ultimately on the long-run performance of the corporation as a whole. Given the remarkable growth in value of GM's common stock during the 1920s, it is reasonable to conclude that GM's bonus plan not

    [38] Brown, "Centralized Control with Decentralized Responsibilities," 8. Mark, "Internal Financial Reporting," 32.
    [39] Sloan, *My Years*, Ch. 7.

only intensified a division manager's desire to stay with the company, but made him eager to comply with company-wide performance goals.[40]

CONCLUSION

The multidivisional structure and management accounting procedures such as the ones devised by GM's top management in the early 1920s have helped giant industrial firms overcome the inefficiency and bureaucratic disabilities that economists once thought were endemic to large-scale organization. In large and diversified enterprises, the multidivisional form of organization sharply reduces the volume of communication, thus enabling managers to employ resources more efficiently and more effectively than if they had continued to use older, centralized forms of organization. New management accounting procedures are indispensable to the successful operation of a multidivisional firm. The internal accounting procedures at GM, for instance, enabled top management to transmit to operating managers in sharp, unambiguous terms its design for company-wide profits and growth. While these procedures impelled all operating managers to pursue the same corporate goals, they also permitted them enormous freedom to exercise initiative in deciding how to employ resources most efficiently. These internal accounting procedures were undoubtedly indispensable to GM's remarkable performance record since 1921. As the number of large firms adopting multidivisional structures in the world increases each year and as public concern about the alleged evils of big business continues to grow, it is clearly imperative to understand the properties of management accounting systems in multidivisional enterprise.

63

[40] *32nd Annual Report of the General Motors Corporation, Year Ended December 31, 1941*, 38–40 and 81. Sloan, *My Years*, 407–420. The Bonus Plan provided "the means to attract and to hold in the employ of the Corporation men of proven and potential ability. . . ." Brown, "Centralized Control with Decentralized Responsibilities," 13. "The Bonus Plan established the concept of corporate profit in place of divisional profits. . . ." Sloan, *My Years*, 409.

II. New Interpretations of Management Accounting History

The Role of Accounting History in the Study of Modern Business Enterprise

H. Thomas Johnson

IT is a truism to observe that one major objective of accounting history is a "better understanding of economic . . . history" (American Accounting Association, 1970, p. 53). Works by accounting historians have long been acknowledged as indispensable to the investigations of economic historians studying Europe and North America from the medieval era to approximately 1850. Indeed, accounting historians and economic historians concentrating upon these early periods often consult the same research materials and ask questions strikingly similar in nature.

This intimate relationship seldom obtains, however, when accounting and economic historians examine the modern age. Economic historians assessing developments from 1850 to the present rarely weigh the findings of accounting historians. Certainly one explanation of the economic historian's indifference to modern accounting history is the increasing sophistication of accounting practices. Only highly trained accounting historians are able to deal with these practices gracefully and perceptively. Although economic historians are capable of recognizing and discussing elementary accounting principles common before the nineteenth century, they are seldom familiar with those complex accounting techniques current since the late 1800's. The work of the economic historian studying the modern era usually ignores, then, the issues and conclusions which would naturally occur to the ac-

counting historian concentrating upon modern history. At times the two fields appear to be as unrelated as C. P. Snow's two cultures. Although the economist and the accountant may not single out the same modern issues and problems for their attention, and although they may not acknowledge the possibility that their modern studies can merge, nevertheless I believe that they can work together effectively to explain the development of American large-scale business firms between 1850 and 1930. The need for cooperative investigation becomes evident if one considers how the typical manufacturing firm of the mid-nineteenth century evolved into those vertically integrated industrial firms that appeared in great numbers during the merger wave of 1897–1903.

It is well known, of course, that typical manufacturing firms of the mid-nineteenth century specialized mainly in one activity: that of transforming raw materials into finished products. These manufacturing firms necessarily relied for nonmanufacturing services upon outside companies that specialized, as did they, primarily in one operation (Chandler and Redlich, 1961). For example, the manufacturer depended upon wholesale suppliers and commission merchants to provide raw materials and to sell finished goods to the

H. Thomas Johnson is Associate Professor, Department of Economics, University of Western Ontario, Canada.

final customer. In that world of specialized firms, "the impersonal forces of supply and demand [governed] the coordination of the flow of goods from the original producer to the final consumer" (Chandler, 1970, p. 56). The vertically integrated industrial firm is quite unlike a mid-nineteenth century firm. The vertically integrated industrial combined into one centrally managed enterprise each specialized activity formerly carried out separately by independent firms. However, in order to control and coordinate these combined activities, the vertically integrated industrial firm had to develop new organizational methods. It is these methods, or structures, which are of particular interest to both the accounting and economic historian.

One new method for controlling and coordinating company procedure was an innovation commonly called "the unitary form of organization." This innovation entailed the creation of independent departments and of one central office to manage both the departments and the entire firm (Williamson, 1970, pp. 10 and 110–12; Chandler, 1966, pp. 43–50). The unitary form of organization also involved the design of complex accounting systems to carry out assessment, operations, and planning throughout the firm. Were accounting historians to conduct extensive analyses of these complicated accounting systems, they would undoubtedly contribute enormously to the economic historian's interpretation of the evolution of America's giant industrial firms. A brief look at the evolution of the E. I. du Pont de Nemours Powder Company suggests how the expertise of the accounting historian is needed to complement the economic historian's work on the development of modern industry since about 1850.

The Du Pont Powder Company exemplifies the early use of accounting data for management control in vertically inte-

grated industrial firms. In order to assess the development of the accounting practices which enabled management to govern the complex operation of this integrated firm, it is useful to know something of the company's background (Chandler and Salsbury, 1971, *passim*). Since 1804 E. I. du Pont de Nemours and Company had engaged primarily in one economic function, the manufacture of explosives. In 1903, however, when three Du Pont cousins purchased this company's assets, thus founding the E. I. du Pont de Nemours Powder Company, they vertically integrated the new firm. After 1903, then, the Du Pont Powder Company was a centrally managed enterprise coordinating through its own departments most of the activities formerly conducted by scores of firms which specialized only in a single operation.

As one might anticipate, a centralized accounting system was indispensable to the Du Pont Powder Company's complex structure (Johnson, 1975). This centralized accounting system needed to accomplish two major objectives: to enable top management to control, coordinate, and assess the horizontal flow of operations among the company's three main departments—manufacturing, sales, and purchasing; and to enable top management to plan the company's long-range development. The first of these objectives was achieved in part because the centralized accounting system coordinated activities among departments by transmitting routine data and instructions. This coordination among departments was complemented by top management control; such control was streamlined as a result of certain accounting procedures. These accounting procedures affected control, for example, by making possible the delegation of responsibility for decisions and daily operations and by generating profit incentives among lower-level management

67

68

and staff. The centralized accounting system permitted more, however, than the control and coordination of activities within the various departments. It also provided routine data which allowed top management to assess each department's operations in terms of management's basic objective—maximum return on investment.

Because the centralized accounting system permitted the coordination, control, and assessment of operations within and among the company's departments, it alleviated the need of time-consuming, demanding attention of top management to daily operations. Once freed from the necessity of making short-term operating decisions, the Powder Company's top management could concentrate on a task relatively unknown in nineteenth century enterprise, the task of planning long-range development. Such planning involved two fundamental activities: the allocation of new investment among competing uses and the financing of new capital requirements. These activities could not be executed without data supplied by the centralized accounting system. This system made available return-on-investment information, cash forecasts, and earnings forecasts. Having established in very general terms the major objectives of the Du Pont Powder Company's centralized accounting system, let us now consider in more detail how this system facilitated short-term operations and long-term planning.

An examination of the uses made of accounting data in the manufacturing, sales, and purchasing departments indicates ways in which the centralized accounting system affected administration of the Powder Company's day-to-day operations. A cost system was the main accounting device that enabled top management to control and assess manufacturing, the largest and most complex of the Powder

Company's operations, involving over forty geographically dispersed mills. Maintained in the home office in Wilmington, Delaware, the centralized cost accounting system compiled full financial information on the cost of goods manufactured. This information was derived in part from home office accounting records and in part from records kept at each mill. Home office payroll and purchasing records supplied wages and raw material costs, while mill production control records provided information on labor, quantities of materials used, and quantities of output produced. Drawing upon all these data, the home office cost department issued separate monthly reports not only for top management, but for each mill superintendent as well.

The monthly reports to superintendents pertained to the physical efficiency of production processes and showed the quantities of raw materials, the dollar costs of labor, and the dollar costs of all other inputs (except administrative overhead) used in every stage of production in each mill. Clearly such data allowed mill superintendents to assume responsibility for daily operational decisions. This responsibility was more limited, however, than would have been the case had the data described the full financial cost of goods manufactured. For example, because their information was only partial, mill superintendents could not make informed "buy or make" decisions.[1] The monthly reports to mill superintendents did encourage them, however, to compete against their own past performance records and those of other mills.

The monthly reports sent by the home office cost department to top management did contain, as one might expect, complete

---

[1] This problem certainly perplexed at least one of the Powder Company's vice-presidents, who felt that mill superintendents should weigh the benefits of purchasing such inputs as acids and wood pulp, products traditionally manufactured by the company.

financial descriptions of product and mill costs. These data enabled top management to make decisions about mill operations in full knowledge of the effect their decisions would have on company profits and return on investment.

Just as centralized accounting procedures were indispensable to the administration of the manufacturing department, so were these procedures essential to the conduct of operations within the Du Pont Powder Company's sales department. Before 1903, the marketing activities of the American explosives industry had been conducted primarily by many independent agents and commission salesmen. Instead of depending upon such decentralized market methods, the Du Pont Powder Company established a large network of branch sales offices across the United States and trained salaried salesmen to move almost all company products. This highly integrated sales department was able to execute its responsibilities successfully—responsibilities which began when goods were finished in the mills and lasted until their delivery to the customer—only because of an effective centralized accounting system. This system provided for control of customer balances, timely appraisal of market trends, and coordination of customer orders with mill production schedules.

Based in part upon the accounting practices of early nineteenth century firms, the Du Pont Company's centralized accounting system, particularly as it affected the sales department, entailed several innovations. One of the most important of these enabled top management to set minimum prices guaranteeing a target rate of return on investment for each product.[2] Because top management was able to fix minimum prices, it could entrust further pricing almost entirely to branch office sales managers. The Du Pont Powder Company's centralized accounting system, in other

words, made it possible for top management to delegate some of the responsibility of making decisions about pricing; thus it minimized considerably what had been, prior to 1903, one of management's major tasks in the explosives industry. Branch office managers were encouraged to set actual prices to customers at levels which, while low enough to discourage new entrants into the industry, were sufficient to allow maximization of total revenue. Indeed, branch managers and their salesmen understood that, if they should bring in a total revenue exceeding that earned merely by selling the required volume at the set minimum price, they would receive a bonus. A bonus incentive system was made available to members of the sales staff, then, as an indirect consequence of the accounting system.

Accounting procedures also aided the administration of daily operations in the purchasing department. Rather than rely upon separate mills to purchase their raw materials, the Powder Company relegated all purchasing of materials to one central purchasing department. A centralized accounts payable voucher system made such an arrangement possible, for it enabled control of the ordering, receiving, and expensing of all raw material purchases. Eventually top management concluded that total reliance upon outside suppliers was ill advised and decided instead to invest capital in the ownership and manufacture of materials required by their company. This decision was based upon careful analysis of expected return from such investment. An investment of this sort (in an outside supply source) was deemed advisable if it seemed likely to yield at least 15% per annum, the return normally earned by the Powder Company's most

69

---

[2] These minimum prices were based, of course, on an expected level of output and expected range of input prices; if either the volume or the cost factor changed, then the minimum price changed accordingly.

70

profitable production activity, dynamite making.

The Powder Company's centralized accounting system did more than provide for the control, coordination, and assessment of short-run operations within the manufacturing, sales, and purchasing departments. In addition, it assisted top management with the task of long-term planning. Long-term planning involved two phases: allocation and financing. Allocation of new investment among competing uses was conducted according to the principle that there "be no expenditures for additions to the earning equipment if the same amount of money could be applied to some better purpose in another branch of the company's business . . . " (Johnson, 1975, p. 4). Return on investment was used to evaluate investment alternatives. Because the centralized accounting system routinely provided information both on net earnings and total investment for each product line and each mill, top management could allocate new investment funds to those products and to those mills that earned the highest return. The Du Pont Powder Company's accounting system enabled top management to carry out another phase of long-term planning, that of financing, by providing monthly forecasts of the company's net earnings and cash position for a year in advance. Since it was the policy of the Du Pont Powder Company to finance its development primarily from retained earnings and sale of common stock, top management required reliable forecasts of net earnings. These forecasts permitted them to determine how much capital would be forthcoming to finance future growth. New long-term capital was needed primarily to construct plant and equipment. An elaborate construction appropriation system advised top management each month for one year in advance of the amounts that would be necessary to cover building outlays. This construction appropriation system and the forecast of net earnings provided the essential information for cash forecasts.

Certainly present-day management accountants are well acquainted with the use of accounting data to plan long-term development and to coordinate, control, and assess short-run operations. When the Du Pont Powder Company followed these practices, however, it was being highly innovative. The uniqueness of the Powder Company's centralized accounting system becomes apparent if one considers some of the most obvious features of accounting systems employed by typical manufacturing firms prior to 1900 (Chandler, 1970, pp. 45–54; Johnson, 1972; Litterer, 1963). Before 1900, routine accounting information seldom guided long-term planning in business firms. On the contrary, the Du Pont Powder Company may well have been the first industrial enterprise to develop an accounting procedure which regularly provided forecasts and other financial information essential to informed long-term planning.

The typical manufacturing firm operating before 1900 apparently expected its accounting system simply to provide information on short-run operations. Cost accounting records were the basic and most highly developed source of such information. Developed first by railroads and textile manufacturers in the 1850's, by the 1890's such cost systems had become quite sophisticated. For example, the little research that has been done on the accounting records of large firms active during the late 1890's in the steel, traction, machine making, and chemical industries suggests that such firms used their relatively advanced cost systems almost exclusively to monitor material and labor costs at the factory level. This emphasis on shop and factory efficiency reflects, of course, the bias of such industrial engineers as Frederick W. Taylor, who designed many of the complex cost systems used by large manufacturing firms during the late nineteenth century.

What is noteworthy in this necessarily brief description of accounting practices in typical manufacturing firms prior to 1900 is the fact that such firms evidently did not concentrate upon commercial efficiency and assessment of overall company performance. Clearly the centralized accounting system of the vertically integrated Du Pont Powder Company was, then, far more sophisticated than accounting procedures adhered to in other firms. The Du Pont Powder Company's system was unique in three fundamental respects: (1) it enabled top management to monitor total financial costs of operations in relation to the company's total performance; (2) it made possible assessment of both operations and overall performance in relation to total investment in productive assets; and (3) it assisted long-term planning decisions.

These remarks about the centralized accounting system employed by the Du Pont Powder Company indicate, I hope, that accounting historians can contribute significantly to the understanding of the development of big business. Accounting historians can very profitably examine the accounting procedures of firms which participated in the merger wave of 1897–1903 and were transformed from executing primarily only one activity, such as manufacturing, to integrating a number of operations. There are two major reasons for encouraging such an investigation. First, the inquiry would indicate how giant enterprises, vertically integrated, are able to function effectively. Many people in the early 1900's believed that large firms such as the Du Pont Powder Company would either topple from the weight of internal inefficiency or would abuse their market power and pass the costs of bureaucratic inefficiency on to the consumer. The record of the past seventy years has disproved this gloomy prediction. Giant enterprise is quite capable of efficient and acceptable behavior. Accounting historians can explain in detail one possible cause of this efficiency.[3] A second reason for the accounting historian's analysis is that, should he help to reveal why large firms operate effectively, he will ultimately provide valuable insight into the relationship between the growth of productivity in the American economy and innovations in the organization of big business.

Economic historians have yet to explain the contribution that innovations in business organization have made both to the growth and to the level of national income per capita in the United States during the past century. Although economists usually agree that improved organizational methods in the business sector of the economy have been responsible for much of the productivity growth in the United States, none has carefully explained these organizational methods (Denison, 1967, pp. 340 and 344; Reynolds, 1973, p. 301). Undoubtedly accounting historians who study the evolution of accounting procedures in large corporations will be able to illuminate the relationship between improved organizational methods and economic growth in this country.

71

[3] It is obvious that accounting systems are part of the administrative structure which affects an organization's efficiency. Although the following works give only cursory treatment to accounting systems *per se*, the relationship between enterprise efficiency and organizational structure is brilliantly analyzed in Chandler, 1966; Chandler and Redlich, 1961; and Williamson, 1970. I believe that accounting historians can add greatly to the understanding of the problems discussed by these authors.

REFERENCES

American Accounting Association, Committee on Accounting History, "Report of the Committee on Accounting History," THE ACCOUNTING REVIEW, Supplement to Vol. XLV (1970), pp. 53–64.

Chandler, Alfred D., Jr., *Strategy and Structure: Chapters in the History of the Industrial Enterprise* (The M.I.T. Press, 1966).

——, *The United States: Evolution of Enterprise* (unpublished ms., September 30, 1970).

—— and Fritz Redlich, "Recent Developments in American Business Administration and Their Conceptualization," *Business History Review* (Spring 1961), pp. 1–31.

—— and Stephen Salsbury, *Pierre S. Du Pont and the Making of the Modern Corporation* (Harper and Row, 1971).

Denison, Edward F., *Why Growth Rates Differ: Postwar Experience in Nine Western Countries* (The Brookings Institution, 1967).

Johnson, H. Thomas, "Early Cost Accounting for Internal Management Control: Lyman Mills in the 1850's," *Business History Review* (Winter 1972), pp. 466–74.

——, "Management Accounting in an Early Integrated Industrial: E. I. du Pont de Nemours Powder Company, 1903–1912," *Business History Review*, XLIX (Summer 1975), pp. 1–28. Page numbers cited refer to the typescript edition which is available from the author on request.

Litterer, Joseph A., "Systematic Management: Design for Organizational Recoupling in American Manufacturing Firms," *Business History Review* (Winter 1963), pp. 369–91.

Reynolds, Lloyd G., *Macroeconomics: Analysis and Policy* (Irwin, 1973).

Williamson, Oliver E., *Corporate Control and Business Behavior: An Inquiry into the Effects of Organization Form on Enterprise Behavior* (Prentice-Hall, 1970).

72

Acknowledgment

This paper was presented to the Fifty-eighth Anniversary Convention of the American Accounting Association in New Orleans, Louisiana on August 19, 1974. I am grateful to Fred Bateman (Indiana University) and Richard B. Du Boff (Bryn Mawr College) for presenting formal comments on this paper to the Convention. I also wish to thank Alfred Chandler (Harvard Business School), Elaine Bowe Johnson (Huron College), and Richard Keehn (University of Wisconsin–Parkside) for helpful comments. Inaccuracies, inconsistencies, and other errors are, of course, my responsibllity.

COMMENTS

by

Fred Bateman   and   Richard B. DuBoff
Graduate School of Business   Department of Economics
Indiana University   Bryn Mawr College
Bloomington, Indiana   Bryn Mawr, Pennsylvania

on

THE ROLE OF ACCOUNTING HISTORY IN THE STUDY

OF MODERN BUSINESS ENTERPRISE

a paper by

H. Thomas Johnson
Department of Economics
University of Western Ontario
London, Canada

Presented to the

Fifty-eighth Anniversary Convention
American Accounting Association
New Orleans, Louisiana
August 19, 1974

COMMENTS ON: "THE ROLE OF ACCOUNTING HISTORY IN THE STUDY OF MODERN
BUSINESS ENTERPRISE," by H. Thomas Johnson

Over the past decade, the technical level of economic history and the
consequent demands on the economic historian's skills have risen dramatically.
The integration of economic theory, statistical analysis and econometrics
into this research field resulted in what has become known as the "new
economic history." This new approach already has provided new insights
into such diverse subjects as the economics of slavery, the market structure
of early American manufacturing, the sources of changing agricultural productivity and the role played by transportation in the process of economic growth.
At professional meetings and in the journals, the list of topics analyzed
expands each year.

Surprisingly, a similar development has not transpired in business
history. Despite the obvious possibilities for technical analysis in the
study of business firms or industries, this field continues to rely almost
completely on historical narrative. Virtually none of the techniques and
tools of the so-called "functional areas"--finance, marketing, management
or accounting--that are taught in most schools of business have found their
way into historical studies of business enterprise nor have those of micro-
economics, the theory of the growth of the firm or location analysis. The
opportunities for a "new business history" seem clear.

These opportunities are well-illustrated by the accounting field, which
it appears to me offers potentially two major contributions. First, the
techniques of accounting and the professional expertise of the accountant
could be applied to the study of firms and industries as they developed, over
time, and indeed to many studies of general economic history as well. Second,

the role played by accounting in the evolution of businesses, particularly
the large-scale corporate firm, needs to be delineated much more specifically than it has in the past. Because of the skill levels required, some
of this work can be accomplished only by accountants who become interested
in historical study. Much, however, can be done in the second category by
economic or business historians willing to strengthen their knowledge of
basic accounting methods.

Let me illustrate the first category by reference to my own work.
With two colleagues, I have been involved in a study of the development of
American manufacturing between 1850 and 1870, the era just preceding that
when the giant industrial corporation began to emerge. We have thus far drawn
upon scientifically-selected samples of individual firm data from the federal
census manuscripts for most of our research, but eventually we intend to examine such sources as corporate records, credit reports and other archival
material. At several points we have searched with little success for articles
or monographs dealing with various aspects of mid-nineteenth century accounting
practices to help clarify some puzzling issues. In our analysis of manufacturing profitability, for example, this lack of supportive literature forced
us to rely upon assumptions rather than upon the solid evidence that accounting
history could have supplied.

Professor Johnson's paper well illustrates the second category, by discussing the centralized accounting system used by the DuPont Company during
that important period in American economic history when business firms were
becoming larger and more complex organizations. For this type of enterprise
virtually no prototypes existed anywhere in the world. American railroads and
a comparatively small number of establishments, among them the DuPont company,
were forced to innovate new techniques in production, management, marketing,

76

finance and accounting. Much has been written about the influences external to the firm, such as the growth of a national market made possible by transportation improvements, that permitted the growth of the large-scale enterprise, but except for the work of a few historians--most notably Alfred Chandler-- very little is known about the relationship between the external and internal changes as viewed from the firm's perspective.

Professor Johnson's paper helps to clarify this relationship with respect to an important internal variable, that of the accounting system. Unfortunately space limitations prevent his providing a more detailed study here, but presumably such work will be forthcoming. Hopefully his paper will also challenge others, accounting or business historians, to initiate similar investigations for other firms. Such work is long overdue.

Fred Bateman
Indiana University

COMMENT ON PAPER BY H. THOMAS JOHNSON

Richard B. DuBoff

Bryn Mawr College

In his sketch of the association between accounting practices
and modern-day corporate enterprise, Professor Johnson laments "the
economic historian's indifference to modern accounting history" and
attributes it to "the increasing sophistication of accounting practices
[which] only highly trained accounting historians are able to deal
with ..."

I agree with this observation about economic historians, but I
take another (not necessarily conflicting) view of their "indifference
to modern accounting history." Over the past 15 years, under the
spell of the "new economic history," there has been a marked trend
away from business history. Much like their Keynesian "new economics"
counterparts, most new economic historians scrupulously avoid coming to
grips with the structure of the American capitalist system and how
its cornerstone -- organized business -- actually operates and
survives. The terrain currently being labored by people like Professor
Johnson is unfamiliar to them, and so they pass it by to carry out
macrostatistical investigations that promise answers to questions
over which there have been decades, if not centuries, of debate (the
economic efficiency of slavery, the contribution of railroads to
economic growth in the nineteenth century, the costs of British

mercantile policies in the eighteenth century, to cite a few).

I do not wish to demean the accomplishments of the new, or quantitative economic history (to which I myself have contributed) so much as I want to call attention to its increasingly obvious inability to throw light upon those institutions that have shaped the society we live in. Johnson's concise account, by contrast, furnishes us with a sort of guide to the transformation of the representative business firm from an inventory liquidator with a modest cost-plus turnover into a large, impersonal, bureaucratized organization whose various parts are tied together by finely calculated cost-minimization criteria.

Centralized accounting, Johnson states, "permitted more ... than the control and coordination of activities within the various departments [of a large vertically integrated corporation]. It also provided routine data which allowed top management to assess each department's operations in terms of management's basic objective -- maximum return on investment." In turn, maximum feasible profits require longer-run planning which "involved two fundamental activities: the allocation of new investment among competing uses and the financing of new capital requirements. These activities could not be executed without data supplied by the centralized accounting system."

Here we have, I believe, an excellent example of selective

disaggregation -- the careful study of individual parts of an
economic system based on the idea that some parts are substantially
more important than others in their impact on the overall level and
nature of economic activity. In other words, Johnson is telling us
not only how modern accounting procedures took root, but that, from
the outset, such procedures embodied accounting with a purpose: the
mutually reinforcing goals of profit growth, sales expansion, and
defensive planning ahead to head off undesirable risks.

Of course, as Professor Johnson himself seems to realize, accounting
structure itself followed business strategy. Modern accounting techniques are designed to help control and coordinate far-flung activities
typical of vertically integrated companies, to determine the cost of
goods manufactured and sold during the course of the year and over
different fiscal periods, and to provide some means (even though
notoriously imperfect) for assigning a monetary value to capital goods.
"Maximization of total revenue," as Johnson repeats, is the great
arbiter -- maximization within constraints, I would add. The DuPont
Company, the focus of Johnson's research, apparently was ahead of
most other firms in the range of its financial information that
facilitated long-term policymaking around 1900, but even by the 1890s
there were "relatively advanced [labor and material] cost systems"
being employed in the steel, chemical, and machinery industries.
What remains to be explored, I would suggest, is exactly what pressures

led firms to innovate in the area of accounting techniques between
1880 and 1905. Some possibilities come to mind: the surging growth
of urban demand, the rise of a national market for industrial
securities, and the increase in speed (as opposed to scale) of
operations and the greater velocity of throughput especially where
manufacturing processes permitted and encouraged vastly greater
applications of mechanical power.

For the still more intrepid, I would offer one more question:
to what extent does profit maximization control both strategy and
structural adaptation? And what are the socioeconomic implications
of the answer to this question? These, for me at least, are the
ultimate issues that flow from the study of the evolution of business
enterprise and modern accounting. For Professor Alfred Chandler,
for instance, functional behavior is merely defined to be that which
adapts an organization (and an accounting system, I presume) to a
strategy assuring its survival. Beyond such economic Darwinism
Chandler treads not. While the rest of us need not -- must not --
be so culture-bound and conservative, we definitely must learn much
more about business structure. For that reason alone the ignorance
of accounting history on the part of economic historians will have
to be reduced.

MARKETS, HIERARCHIES, AND THE HISTORY

OF MANAGEMENT ACCOUNTING

by

H. Thomas Johnson

Professor of Accounting

Western Washington University

Bellingham, Washington, 98225

July, 1980

Prepared for the

Third International Congress of Accounting Historians,

London Business School

London, England, August 16-18, 1980

MARKETS, HIERARCHIES, AND THE HISTORY

OF MANAGEMENT ACCOUNTING

Abstract

Accountants have recently perceived that knowledge about the internal economics of hierarchical and market forms of organization will undoubtedly expand our understanding of management accounting in contemporary business firms. This paper demonstrates that such knowledge also provides significant insight into the historical development of management accounting practice in complex business organizations. Between approximately 1800 and 1930, as will be seen, the continued development of new management accounting practices occurred because American business organizations were trying to lower the cost of conducting economic activity in increasingly large and complex hierarchical structures by developing new accounting information systems to aid decision-making and control.

MARKETS, HIERARCHIES, AND THE HISTORY OF
MANAGEMENT ACCOUNTING

I.   Introduction

   Today it is widely recognized that management accounting systems vary to
provide whatever financial information a business organization requires in order to plan
and control its operations. The dynamic adaptability of management accounting has been
carefully documented in historical studies describing how nineteenth- and early
twentieth-century American business firms continually altered their internal accounting
procedures to suit changed conditions. Although accountants have noted that particular
alterations in management accounting practice accompany changes either in business
firms themselves or in the external environment of those firms, they have no theory to
explain why this should be the case. This paper will examine the relationship between
changes in management accounting practice and changes in economic activities in order
to show that certain kinds of historical developments in management accounting systems
necessarily accompanied certain changes in American businesses.

   As a prelude to this investigation, it should be noted that discussions of the role of
accounting in business organizations have not adequately explained how dynamic change
within a firm or within its environment produces change in its management accounting
system [cf. Cooper, 1951; Amey and Egginton, 1973, ch. 13]. Research accountants have
tended to focus, while relying largely upon information-economic theories and
contingency theories, either upon overly-simplified, abstract cases or else upon static
representations of a specific information system [Spicer and Ballew, pp. 2-8]. Recently,
however, economists have developed a general theory to explain the various systems that
society uses to organize economic activity. Specifically, these economists have explored
the question of why society organizes some economic activity through the "invisible
hand" of decentralized market systems and other economic activity through the "visible
hand" of hierarchical administration systems (such as large business firms) [Alchian and
Demsetz, 1972; Williamson, 1975; Caves, 1980; Marris and Mueller, 1980]. As some
accountants have recently perceived, knowledge about the internal economics of
hierarchical and market forms of organization will surely expand our understanding of
management accounting in contemporary business firms [Amey and Egginton, 1973, chs.
13 and 18; Spicer and Ballew, 1980, pp. 9-40]. The objective of this paper is to
demonstrate that this knowledge will also provide significant insights into the historical
development of internal management accounting practice in complex business
organizations.

II.   Markets, Hierarchies and Management Accounting

   A thorough analysis of the evolution of internal management accounting practice
requires familiarity with the economic theory mentioned in part I. Recently developed
by economists to explain the systems society employs to organize economic activity, this
theory claims that society relies essentially upon two basic methods to organize
economic activity. It operates either through decentralized market systems in which
autonomous entities conduct transactions, or through centralized hierarchical systems in
which a single administrative entity spans both sides of transactions [Alchian and
Demsetz, 1972; Williamson, 1975, p. xi]. Market prices supply the information needed to
make decisions in a market setting, including those decisions which an administrative
entity makes regarding activities it conducts through the market [Arrow, 1963, p. 403].
One does not need accounting procedures, of course, to gather information about market
prices. Although businesses from the early Middle ages to the late eighteenth century
kept double-entry accounts, they did so primarily to record claims and debts arising from

85

- 1 -

final market transactions, and not to gather information for decision-making [Chatfield, 1974, pp. 58-61]. Market prices supply only part of the information required when an administrative entity conducts economic activity internally. The effective and efficient conduct of internal economic activity can be assessed by an administrative entity only if it possesses other sources of information, particularly a management accounting system.

Although it is self-evident that administrative systems require internal accounting information to function properly, scholars have yet to elaborate a comprehensive economic and organizational theory which explains the link between accounting information practices and the growth of large-scale administrative entities [cf. Cooper, 1951; Galbraith, 1972]. Until very recently, economists seldom studied hierarchical institutions. Rather, they attended almost exclusively to the formal properties of purely competitive market systems [Williamson, 1975, pp. 250-251; Leibenstein, 1979, pp. 477-478; Simon, 1979]. Two prominent exceptions, however, are Ronald Coase and Oliver Williamson, economists who have serious pondered why firms exist and why they grow. An examination of their ideas is essential to an understanding of how the growth of hierarchically administered business firms creates a demand for internally generated financial information.

Ronald Coase was probably the first economist to observe that conventional price theory, drawn to its logical conclusion, contradicts reality: it fails to provide for the existence of business firms as they are actually known to us today. In a remarkable article written over forty years ago, Coase [1937] noted that if market prices transmit information efficiently, as conventional theory supposes they do, then the economy should consist entirely of one-member sub-units which conduct all economic activity via market exchange. In reality, however, the economy contains a great many multi-member sub-units, such as business firms, which conduct at least some of society's economic activity via administrative means. Coase accounted for the existence of these firms by assuming that markets must be costly (because imperfect) systems for transmitting at least some types of information [Marris and Mueller, 1980, p. 36]. Working from this assumption, he deduced that firms exist because they provide a system for transmitting certain information and for organizing certain economic activity at lower cost than the market. Coase concluded that society will distribute economic activity between markets and hierarchies until the marginal cost of organizing activity within each administrative entity equals the marginal cost of organizing activity within the market system.

Although Coase provided a theoretical explanation for the observed coexistence of markets and hierarchies, he did not identify the causes of the information-transmission costs which determine how society distributes economic activity between markets and hierarchies [Alchian and Demsetz, 1972, pp. 783-784; Williamson, 1975, pp. 3-4]. Writing in the 1970's, however, economist Oliver Williamson has identified many of the "frictions" that make information transmission costly in both markets and hierarchies [Marris and Mueller, 1980, p. 37; Williamson, 1973 and 1975]. Williamson's studies are so far the most ambitious attempt by an economist to explain the internal dynamics of entreprise growth and development. A brief explanation of the costs Williamson associates with economic activity in markets and hierarchies is essential to a clear understanding of how management accounting developed.

Williamson attributes those information-transmission costs identified by Coase to bounded rationality and opportunism. "Bounded rationality" refers to man's limited ability to solve complex and uncertain problems. Were his rationality not limited, man could settle complex and uncertain economic problems through the market and at zero cost simply by negotiating long-term contracts which "identify future contingencies and specify, ex ante, appropriate adapations thereto" [Williamson, 1975, p. 9]. The cost that bounded rationality actually does impose on long-term contracting could conceivably be circumvented by organizing complicated and uncertain problems in the market with recurrent short-term contracts. Such contracts could be renegotiated whenever unexpected contingencies developed. Recurrent short-term market contracting is precluded, however, by opportunism. The human tendency to pursue self interest with deceitful strategies inevitably makes short-term market contracting costly and risky, particularly if the number of participants in the market is small [Williamson, 1975, pp. 26-30 and 124].

Just as bounded rationality and opportunism prevent cost-free arrangement of economic activity in the market place, so do they impose costs upon attempts to organize economic activity within administrative entities. In an administrative unit, however, if large-scale, complex, and highly uncertain economic activities are being organized, often costs will be less (at the margin) than they will be in the market system. Costs may be less primarily because administrative entities, unlike the market system, have a wide array of control machinery and incentive devices (embodied in many cases in the management accounting system) which encourage employees to suppress opportunism and to pursue activities which conform to the goals of the organization itself [Williamson, 1975, pp. 39-40 and 253-258]. A firm can provide, furthermore, a sense of esprit that is more conducive to joint profit-maximization than is the calculating spirit pervading most markets [Williamson, 1975, pp. 37-39; Clague, 1977].

The curtailment of opportunism enables an administrative entity to take full advantage of its ability to factor complex problems into several interdependent parts which managers can handle one by one. Sequential decision-making, that is to say "the internal organizational counterpart to short-term contracting" which administrative entities permit [Williamson, 1975, pp. 9-10 and 124], can succeed because opportunism is kept from interfering with managerial responsibilities. Managers are sufficiently freed from a concern with opportunism to solve complex and uncertain tasks by separating them into interdependent parts to be handled as they arise. Such an approach to tasks, moreover, alleviates the consequences of limited rationality. Factoring of complex problems into smaller ones eliminates the need to anticipate from the outset all possible contingencies. Man's bounded rationality therefore ceases to be an insurmountable liability.

Factoring, possible once opportunism is contained and a procedure well-suited to the limitations of man's mind, is nevertheless difficult to practice successfully. For factoring itself creates the problem that the performance of myriad sub-units within a firm's administrative system may not always conform to the goals of the organization as a whole. Because of the possibility of a discrepancy between the organization's goals and the performance of sub-units, a structure is required to integrate the specialized and differentiated activities of a firm's subdivided units into a cohesive entity capable of achieving system-wide benefits. Structure, as that term is used here, refers not only to the design that is used to coordinate the interdependent activities of a firm's component parts, but also to the systems (such as the management acccounting system) which transmit information throughout the structure [Chandler, 1966, p. 16; Lawrence and Lorsch, 1969, ch. 1; Galbraith, 1972].

Although structural changes may take many forms, organization theorists observe that the choice of structure is dictated primarily by the amount of uncertainty surrounding a firm's tasks.[1] Because "task uncertainty require[s] information processing during the execution of the task," therefore "in order to be effective, an organization must design a structure which is capable of processing the amount of information

---

[1] The ideas in this paragraph are drawn from Galbraith [1972]; the passages quoted above come from page 72.

required by the task. The organization can take action either to reduce the amount of information required or to increase the capacity of the structure to process more information." Jay Galbraith notes in this regard that an organization can reduce the amount of information required to coordinate increasingly interdependent tasks among its sub-units either by"adding slack resources" or by changing the "authority structure to a more self-contained form." Although both strategies decrease interdependence among the firm's component parts, the former one "maintains a centralized decision-making process," while the latter decentralizes decision-making "down to where the information exists." A firm can increase the capacity of its structure to process more information either by adopting procedures that "reduce the time between successive planning sessions" or by creating "lateral relations between interdependent sub-units." The first strategy "brings information up to the decision makers and results in centralization of decisions," while the second "brings decision making lower in the organization and therefore results in decentralization." Galbraith's observations bear on consideration of the following postulate: namely, if a firm is to take advantage of changes in the economic or technological environment, then it must integrate into its system increasingly complex and interdependent economic tasks. In order to accomplish such integration, it is essential, as Galbraith implies, that the firm select a structure certain to process the information necessitated by this increased uncertainty.

The internal accounting information required by three well-known types of structures —the elemental multi-process structure, the centralized unitary structure, and the decentralized multi-divisional structure — is examined in the following historical sections of this paper. Each structure is associated with those changes in markets or technologies which made entrepreneurs deem it profitable to increasingly integrate economic activities into administrative entities [Chandler and Redlich, 1961]. The following discussion also considers the accounting changes that accompanied each new type of structure. In so doing, it reveals how those changes enabled each type of structure to efficiently organize (as efficiently as can be done by the market system or a competing firm) complex and uncertain economic activities.

III. Management Accounting in Large-Scale American Business Firms, 1800-1930.

In 1800, virtually all economic activity in the United States was conducted by individuals and small groups through market exchange. By 1930, however, a commanding share of the nation's economic activity was carried on within administrative entities, some of which had annual expenditures greater than the national products of most nations. From 1800 to 1930 were developed virtually all the kinds of administrative structures now in existence. During those years, as recent studies by business historians point out, business firms developed - - in response to changes in markets and technology which made it profitable to integrate increasing amounts of economic activity into their administrative systems - - three basic types of administrative organizations. The following sections discuss the development of each of these three kinds of organization and explain the changes each type of organization brought to management accounting practice.

A. Single-activity, multi-process firms

From about 1800 to 1890, business firms specializing in single activities such as production, transportation, or distribution developed hierarchical systems with which to administer collections of distinct processes.[1] Specializing in production, for example,

----

[1] Activity is synonymous with function, a term often used by organization theorists. A process is one of several elemental tasks which comprise an activity. For example, manufacturing bread is an activity which includes mixing and baking as two processes.

early nineteenth-century textile mills were probably the first entities to use internal administrative procedures to coordinate manufacturing processes. Using similar procedures to coordinate internal processes, giant mass-production enterprises succeeded near the end of the century in converting raw materials into finished goods on an unprecedented scale. Railroad firms by mid century had also devised complex procedures to administer a multitude of processes involved in shipping goods and people over land. Finally, by the 1880's urban retailers and mail-order houses had coordinated the mass distribution of goods between producers and consumers [Chandler, 1977].

All these nineteenth-century, single-activity enterprises — textile mills, railroads, mass producers, and mass distributors — required internal financial information to control the internal coordination of processes which previously the market system had coordinated. They still relied, of course, on market price information to guide decisions about their exchanges with outsiders such as suppliers of inputs or purchasers of goods and services. But these single-activity enterprises had to synthesize financial information with which to monitor the efficiency of internally administered economic processes. And for that, they created management accounting systems.

The first evidence of modern management accounting occurs in early nineteenth-century textile mills, appearing in special accounts designed to gather information about direct costs of internally administered processes (such as carding, spinning, weaving and finishing). To appreciate the significance of these early manufacturing cost accounts, one must understand that the first textile mills appeared because merchant-entrepreneurs realized that the opportunities presented by expanding world markets for cotton cloth and by the new water- and steam-power technologies devised for spinning and weaving could not be captured effectively with conventional market-mediated methods of production. The "cottage industry" system of domestic production, for instance, simply would not suffice. In order to profit from those opportunities, then, entrepreneurs transferred from the domestic system to the centralized factory system the processes used to convert raw fiber into yarn and fabric [Chapman, 1974]. As a result of that transfer, an administered hierarchy, the mill, coordinated numerous conversion processes which in the domestic system had been linked through autonomous market exchanges. To monitor the efficiency of mill-coordinated processes, and particularly to gauge the productivity of workers now paid a wage instead of a piece-rate, managers devised what are known today as manufacturing cost accounts. These accounts provided detailed information about direct conversion costs in every process of a mill's production system [Johnson, 1972; Stone, 1973; Porter, 1980].

The managers of early textile mills used information from these nascent cost records to make short-run decisions and to achieve control in the one aspect of their operation not governed by market exchange prices: namely, the conversion of raw materials into finished goods. Competitive market prices beyond the manager's control dictated, of course, the exchange rates for finished goods, for raw materials, for supplies, and for the laborer's time. The mill manager himself, however, could influence the rate at which laborers, using other inputs, converted raw cotton into yarn or fabric. Information from accounts about the cost of that conversion process aided the manager's task of evaluation and control. Such information included the conversion cost per pound of output by department for each worker and for each type of direct overhead expense. Using contribution margin information derived from these conversion costs, mill foremen and marketing officials in early cotton textile companies frequently made decisions about special-order prices and equipment modifications [Johnson, 1972, p. 474].

89

Even greater than the demand for internal accounting information created by early textile mills was the demand generated by the complex administrative problems which American railroads faced after mid-century. The creation of large railroad companies by entrepreneurs wishing to capture the profits made possible by new iron and steam-power technologies marked the advent of "big business" [Chandler, 1977, pp. 80-89]. While harnessing the new technologies of iron and steam to reduce transportation costs, these mid-century railroads grew to sizes that dwarfed the scale of even the largest textile factories. Managing these giant transportation entities was an unprecedented task. But by 1870 several railroad administrators had devised ingenious solutions which became the core of modern administrative practice. Indeed, Alfred D. Chandler, Jr.'s important studies of 19th century railroad administration document the path-breaking role of railroads in resolving many of the problems of management, finance, labor relations, competition and government regulations that faced giant enterprises in industrial sectors after 1900 [Porter, 1973, p. 31]. Among the solutions achieved by railroads were, of course, internal accounting systems designed to provide the financial information required to manage large-scale administrative entities.

90
American railroads made two major contributions to management accounting practice during the nineteenth century [Chandler, 1977, pp. 109-120 and 186]. First they developed systems that not only kept track of enormous numbers of transactions but also that summarized the result of the transactions for timely and efficient reporting. Railroads handled a vastly greater number and dollar volume of transactions than had any previous business. To control and keep account of receipts from passengers and shippers, for instance, required systems both for collecting and depositing cash daily at hundreds of different locations spread over a vast geographic area and also for prompt reporting and transfer of funds to headquarter offices. To accomplish this, railroads led the way in developing pre-numbered ticket and invoice procedures, in using imprest cash funds, and in using the telegraph to transfer both funds and information. To monitor expenditures of money, the railroads also required new accounting systems: they needed methods to control disbursements of cash and also to record disbursements in efficient ways that gave management timely and accurate reports on types of expenditures. The railroads solved the problems of controlling and recording disbursements by devising what accountants know today as the voucher system of bookkeeping.

Railroads did more, however, than develop record-keeping systems that provided an orderly accumulation of voluminous financial transactions and a way to rapidly and systematically report financial affairs for many sub-units within a large and geographically widespread organization. American railroads in the nineteenth century also pioneered in devising summary accounting statistics necessary for evaluating and controlling the operating performance of their complex and diverse sub-units. To compare performance, for instance, among sub-units and among classes of services which had very different capital intensities or very different rates of operation, certain railroads by the 1860's and 1870's were compiling statistics such as the cost per ton-mile. Moreover, railroads were the first modern businesses to use broad financial statistics to assess the performance of a company. Among such statistics, the railroads especially favored the operating ratio, a comparison of operating income with sales that resembles today's contribution margin ratio.

Between 1870 and about 1895 there appeared two other types of single-activity organizations. One type was engaged in manufacturing, and the other in distribution. In order to run their own large-scale operations, both types of organization copied administrative practices from the railroads. As had the textile factories and the railroads before them, these two types of organization arose in response to new technologies. For the new technologies made it possible to coordinate certain economic activities more efficiently within an administrative hierarchy than within existing market systems. Wholesale and retail distributors (e.g., mail order houses, department stores and chain stores) took advantage of new technologies in transportation and communication - - embodied primarily in the railroad and the telegraph - - to reach masses of customers within wide regional and national boundaries [Chandler, 1977, ch. 7]. Similarly, manufacturers took advantage of new technologies in metal-making and heat generation to mass-produce myriad products such as iron and steel, petroleum distillates, alcoholic beverages, chemicals, processed foods, farm implements and metal machinery [Chandler, 1977, ch. 8]. These new types of large-scale organizations continued to rely on the market system to purchase their basic inputs (either finished merchandise or raw materials) and, in the case of manufacturers, to sell finished products to customers. They relied on their internal administrative system to coordinate multiple processes involving one basic activity: conversion of raw materials into finished goods in the case of mass-producers, and distribution of finished goods to consumers in the case of mass-marketers. Because each firm administered only one basic activity, these organizations resembled both textile factories (converters) and railroads (transporters). But the speed of throughput in these late nineteenth-century manufacturing and distributing organizations enabled them to attain sizes more reminiscent of the railroads than of textile mills. Because of the magnitude of these companies, their founders usually turned to the railroads for ideas and for trained administrative personnel.

Mass-distributors and mass-producers compiled for controlling and evaluating their own multiple processes accounting information similar to the cost per ton-mile and the operating ratios which railroad administrators used to control and evaluate the myriad components of their giant transportation systems [Chandler, 1977, chs. 7 and 8; Chandler and Daems, 1979]. Both the manufacturers and the distributors relied on variants of the operating ratio to assess and control the overall performance of their respective organizations [Chandler, 1977, pp. 223 and 268]. Neither used the cost per ton-mile, of course, to gauge the efficiency with which they coordinated their particular internal processes. Many mass-production manufacturing firms instead compiled very detailed accounting information about direct conversion and raw material costs within myriad sub-units of their organizations [Chandler, 1977, pp. 246, 257-258 and 268]. Mass-distributing firms, on the other hand, resorted to compiling sales turnover statistics by department and by sales area as a means of gauging the efficiency of their internally-coordinated processes [Chandler, 1977, pp. 223, 227-229, and 235-236].

It is noteworthy that apparently none of these nineteenth-century large-scale, single-activity organizations - - railroads, mass-distributors, or mass-production manufacturers - - developed internal accounting information with which to assess how effectively a company employed capital [Johnson, 1975, p. 188]. Even though many of these organizations employed vast quantities of fixed plant and equipment, they designed internal accounting systems only to provide management with financial information about the internal efficiency of various processes which converted inputs into output. It is not surprising, however, that certain entrepreneurs should direct their attention to accounting information from the "shop floor." Those such as Nathan Appleton in textiles, Albert Fink in railroads, Andrew Carnegie and John D. Rockefeller in manufacturing, and Marshall Field in retailing, all of whom designed administrative systems intended to integrate economic processes more efficently than could the market system, especially sought such information. Most late nineteenth-century exponents of "scientific management," such as F. W. Taylor, also identified a top manager's main concerns primarily with the level of the shop (i.e., process), rather than with the level of the enterprise as a whole [Johnson, 1975, pp. 193-194; Wren, 1979, pp. 131-135; Jelinek, 1980]. Indeed, entrepreneurs and management experts (with the exception of A. H. Church [Jelinek, 1980]) both took for granted the capital invested in a large-scale, single-activity organization. They devoted their attention primarily to managing as efficiently as possible the separate processes in which the organization's capital was embodied; for that purpose, accounting information on stock turnover or direct conversion costs was sufficient.

The records of large-scale, single activity firms that appeared during the late 1800's omit several types of management accounting information which, today, managers of such organizations would consider indispensable. The first thing a modern accountant would miss in the records of late nineteenth-century business is careful, consistent allocation of fixed capital costs to products and/or to periods. Periodic income statements, such as they were, showed little concern either for asset depreciation or for full absorption product costing [Brief, 1965; Chatfield, 1974, pp. 101-102 and 159-160]. It is not surprising, then, that balance sheets seldom contained meaningful figures for costs or values of fixed assets and inventories, although in most cases balance sheets were prepared more thoroughly than were income statements [Littleton, 1933, pp. 236 and 245; Johnson, 1972, p. 474]. Another thing modern accountants would find missing in the records of these single-activity organizations operating near the close of the previous century is accounting information with which to plan and control large capital investments [Chandler, 1977, pp. 186, 223, 238, 258, 268, 274, and 279]. Despite the increased uncertainty which accompanies long-term commitments of capital, these firms apparently used no forecasts or capital budgets to coordinate and monitor investment outlays.[1] There is no evidence, furthermore, that they used accounting information such as return on investment either to select (ex ante) or to evaluate (ex post) investment projects [Johnson, 1975, p. 188].

The omission by enormous single-activity business firms of several types of management accounting information deemed by modern accountants to be essential to administering a capital-intensive entity apparently created no serious obstacles. These nineteenth-century firms apparently did not require special accounting information to judge how effectively they had used capital in the particular environment they faced. One thing that greatly reduced the need to make frequent public reports on their financial condition was their overwhelming reliance on internal sources of new capital. Undoubtedly, the enormous expansion of markets in late nineteenth-century America also helped reduce the uncertainty associated with long-term investment and, in so doing, lessened the need for costly planning and budgeting systems. Finally, the fact that each nineteenth-century railroad, manufacturing, or distributing firm engaged in only one basic activity meant that the firm really could choose between only two alternative uses for new capital: the firm itself or an outside firm (or investment). Presumably most firms in the late 1800's ruled out the last alternative because to select it would be tantamount to admitting managerial failure. That left the firm itself. And because the firm engaged exclusively in one activity, it did not need internal accounting information (such as return on investment) to decide where to put new capital. The firm had only to know how new investment would affect the turnover ratios or the unit conversion costs in processes where capital was intended to go. Adequate for that purpose was the information supplied in most late nineteenth-century management accounting systems.

B.   Multi-activity firms.

The budgeting, forecasting, return on investment, and other types of management accounting procedures not used by single-activity firms in the late 1800's did appear soon after 1900. These procedures were adopted by the new vertically integrated industrial

----

[1] Railroads might have begun capital budgeting by the 1890's except that government regulation of rate making and diminution of competition helped reduce uncertainty and, therefore, the need to plan [Chandler and Redlich, 1961].

firms that appeared in large numbers during merger waves around the turn of the century. These firms combined in one administrative entity two or more primary activities such as manufacturing, distributing, purchasing, or transportation [Chandler, 1977, Part IV]. Many of the names of the vertically integrated multi-activity, industrial giants that appeared around 1900 became familiar household items in the twentieth century: for example, Standard Oil of New Jersey, International Harvester, Singer Sewing Machine, DuPont, United Fruit, National Biscuit, and General Electric.

The entrepreneurs who created these organizations perceived that in some industries the flow of economic activity between mass-producers and mass-distributors could be coordinated more efficiently within an administrative hierarchy than within existing market institutions. This coordination within an administrative hierarchy was especially possible in industries where existing networks of distributors could not vent high volumes of new mass-produced commodities (e.g., sewing machines, dynamite, specialized electrical machinery, kerosene, refrigerated foods and complex farm machinery). In instances where existing markets did not enable a single-activity firm to capture fully the economies inherent in either high speed mass-production or high speed mass-distribution, entrepreneurs extended the visible hand of administrative control from the various processes comprising a single economic activity to the various activities comprising an entire industry [Chandler, 1977, pp. 285-286].

93

Although vertically integrated, multi-activity organizations promised the nation's consumers more goods and services at lower costs than had ever been known before, in actuality these organizations often found it difficult to realize their potential. Because of the complexity and diversity of their activities, the vertically integrated organization strained the bounds of managerial rationality and encouraged opportunistic behavior more than had any administrative entities in history. Indeed, many observers predicted in the early 1900's that the bureaucratic inefficiency of these vertically integrated, industrial giants would topple them. Many of these firms evidently avoided internal chaos and collapse largely as a result of organizational innovations, including new management accounting procedures, which compensated for bounded rationality and curtailed possibilities for the opportunistic conduct invited by largeness and complexity within an organization [Williamson, 1979, p. vii and ch. 1].

To make tractable the task of managing a vertically integrated organization, a new type of administrative structure had to be devised which could deal with the uncertainty inherent in coordinating diverse activities. The structure adopted by the most successful vertically integrated giants is known today as the unitary form of organization [Williamson, 1970, ch. 2; Chandler, 1966, pp. 43-50]. The unitary organization factors the operations of each distinct activity into separate departments (e.g., a department for selling, one for manufacturing, one for transportation, and so forth); and it creates one central office both to coordinate the departments and to direct their diverse activities toward common goals. The unitary structure is the natural way to arrange diverse, interdependent activities because, as organizational theorists point out, this structure allows for two degrees of management specialization: some managers concentrate on economic performance within each department, while others concentrate on coordinating the performances of the various departments of the firm as a unit [Williamson, 1975, p. 133]. Each department is managed by a specialist who can use all the techniques of steady-state management, techniques which, by 1900, were highly developed and thoroughly publicized by writers such as F. W. Taylor [Litterer, 1963]. Given this system, each department can strive, as though it were a separate, single-activity company, for cost efficiencies and scale economies. Furthermore, top management, freed from the task of operating separate departments, can apply its bounded capacities to attaining peak coordination and achieving for the company's combined operation costs and profits superior to anything that could be realized by the separate parts of the company were they organized either through the market or through another competing administrative entity.

The successful attainment of its goals by a typical unitary organization depends in part, however, on how effectively it deals with a problem attendant upon the very diversity and complexity of its activities. Such complex and varied activities permit department heads and their subordinates to pursue sub-goals. By definition these sub-goals conflict with the ultimate aims of top management. Opportunities to pursue sub-goals exist for two main reasons. Their bounded rationality makes top managers incapable of exercising infallible control, and man's inherent opportunism lures employees to distort instructions or information [Williamson, 1970, ch. 2; 1975, ch.7]. The result of these conditions is control loss, which Williamson characterizes as the organizational counterpart of market transaction costs. Although control loss is an inescapable consequence of human frailty, its adverse impact on the growth and efficiency of a vertically integrated organization can be mitigated by the creation of appropriate systems for transmitting information and instructions within a unitary structure.

Designed to mitigate control loss and the pursuit of sub-goals within a unitary form of organization is the remarkable management accounting system created between about 1903 and 1915 by the founders of the E. I. DuPont de Nemours Powder Company [Johnson, 1975]. The DuPont Powder Company was the vertically integrated successor to the well-known family firm that had manufactured gunpowder and explosives in the United States since 1804. The original single-activity, manufacturing firm always acquired raw materials and sold finished products through market exchanges with other firms. The DuPont Powder Company of 1903, however, combined the original family manufacturing firm with other manufacturing firms that produced high explosives and dynamite. It integrated these varied manufacturing activities into one giant organization that also included both a national sales network and a large raw material purchasing department. To manage its diverse activities, the company's founders devised a unitary structure with one central office in Wilmington, Delaware, and separate departments for each of the major activities: manufacturing, marketing, and purchasing.

An elaborate management accounting system did a great deal to reduce control loss and sub-goal pursuit within the DuPont Company's unitary structure. At the heart of the system, the company used an accounting proxy for market efficiency — return on investment — to establish an enterprise-wide goal for planning and control. Return on investment served not only as a measure of financial performance for the company as a whole, but also as a uniform financial yardstick for measuring performance in each of the company's diverse departments. Using the same criterion to evaluate and control each department's disparate activities reduced the amount of information required by top management to control the company's complex operations. This reduction had the effect of strengthening and enlarging top management's span of control. Moreover, measuring each department's separate performance in terms of the company's comprehensive financial objective also reduced the scope for sub-goal pursuits by departmental managers.

In addition to its use of return on investment, the internal accounting system in operation at DuPont by about 1915 is also distinguished by its methods of analyzing return on investment. It examines return on investment in terms of the operating ratio and the sales turnover ratio which single-activity firms employed in the late nineteenth century to measure financial performance. The analysis is embodied in the famous equation developed by Donaldson Brown in approximately 1912 for the Treasurer's Office at DuPont [Johnson, 1978, p. 508]. In that equation, $R = P \times T$, return on investment is equated to the product of the operating ratio (P) and the sales to capital turnover ratio (T). DuPont's well-known "chart system" provides detailed information from each of the company's departments for every item in the income statement that affects the operating ratio and for every item in the balance sheet that affects turnover [Davis, 1950]. Because all of the controllable factors affecting return on investment are disaggregated in this fashion, top management can use the chart system to compare budgeted targets with actual performance each month in every department.

By an ingenious use of return on investment, then, the DuPont organization used conventional measures of financial performance corresponding to each of the company's separate activities, and yet avoided the narrow "shop-floor" view of top management's role that often pervaded single-activity enterprises before 1900. In retrospect it seems natural that top managers in a vertically integrated enterprise - - an enterprise created, ostensibly, to coordinate diverse economic activities more efficiently than the market coordinates them - - should give priority to the combined performance of the enterprise's parts acting jointly rather than to the separate performance of individual parts. At the turn of the century, however, few people had encountered vertically integrated business systems, and fewer still had tried to articulate an accounting information system with which to control the activities in a centralized unitary structure. With no obvious precedent to follow, then, members of the DuPont organization between about 1903 and 1915 created a management accounting system for controlling performance which remains to this day a model copied by complex business organizations.

Implicit in the accounting information system used by the DuPont Company to control financial performance is a broad conception of top management's role. Similarly, the accounting procedures the company adopted to help management make decisions about new capital investments reflects the same broad view of top management's responsibility [Johnson, 1975, pp. 187-190]. The DuPont Company developed an elaborate system for forecasting to derive information about sources of new capital. Indeed, theirs was probably the first accounting system for forward planning used by an American industrial firm. Starting with a forecast of sales in each segment of its market for a year ahead, the company projected net earnings, cash position, and available capital by month. Top management could select among alternative uses of capital according to the rule that there "be no expenditures for additions to the earning equipment if the same amount of money could be applied to some better purpose in another branch of the company's business" [quoted in Johnson, 1975, p. 187]. The criterion used by top management to evaluate projects was, of course, return on investment. Judging the best use of new capital dollars required knowing, therefore, the expected earning power and capacity constraints of each separate department. The company's departmental return on investment reports, together with departmental budget forecasts, supplied the necessary information.

Unlike the DuPont Company, large-scale, single-activity firms operating during the nineteenth century apparently compiled no systematic accounting information for capital budgeting. And yet this omission does not necessarily indicate that administrators of these early firms failed to allocate capital responsibly. On the contrary, it probably indicates that before 1900 the benefits to most single-activity organizations of additional information about internal efficiency of capital did not warrant the cost of maintaining elaborate forecasting and budgeting procedures. The diverse array of activities in a vertically integrated firm presented top management, however, with capital budgeting alternatives that were too complex to be evaluated completely without special financial information. The information they had at their disposal enabled DuPont executives to choose rationally among diverse alternatives that included many different types of products, various regional markets in the nation, and numerous opportunities to make or buy raw material inputs.

C.   Multi-division firms.

The return on investment information used by multi-activity, vertically integrated firms to measure performance and to allocate capital provided the founders of the first multi-division enterprises with a cornerstone upon which to base their management accounting systems. Emerging in the United States shortly after World War I [Chandler, 1966; Chandler and Redlich, 1961], the new, multi-division firms did not precipitate any major changes in, or departures from, the types of management accounting procedures already used in multi-activity, vertically integrated firms. Indeed the multi-division structure is essentially a single administrative entity that is designed to coordinate the operations of two or more multi-activity units. But the multi-division structure focuses management's attention on profit goals more intently than do either single- or multi-activity structures [Williamson, 1970, ch. 8; 1975, p. 150]. It therefore increases the importance placed by the internal accounting system on company-wide measures of profit such as return on investment.

The particular changes brought by the multi-division form of organization eliminated the very inefficiencies which multi-activity organizations encountered when they diversified either the array of products or the geographic areas encompassed by their administrative systems [Johnson, 1978, p. 491]. According to Chandler [1966], when multi-activity companies such as DuPont, Sears Roebuck, and General Motors diversified after World War I, they discovered that their unitary structures did not suffice for the management of diverse product lines or sales areas. The centralized unitary structure necessitated, of course, that top management itself not only coordinate all of a firm's operating activities (production, distribution, transportation, and so forth), but that it also plan the firm's long-term growth and development. When multi-activity companies diversified, then, top management was burdened with a voluminous and complex flow of internal communications. Overwhelmed by the inordinate demands made upon it, top management could neither coordinate the firm's daily operating activities nor plan its long-run policies.

Eventually, leaders of giant, diversified companies learned that decentralization of operations management and centralization of plan management would assure the efficient operation of their organizations. Decentralization was achieved by isolating into semi-autonomous divisions the multiple activities of each product or of each geographic region. The operations of each division, comprising in effect the operations of an entire multi-activity, vertically integrated organization, were then placed under the jurisdiction of a division manager. A division manager became responsible for coordinating and controlling all operating activities for one product line or sales region. The only restraints on his authority were the policies and goals established by top management for the company as a whole. Top management, relieved of responsibility for coordinating the operating activities of various divisions, could concentrate exclusively on planning company-wide policy and assuring that the performance of each division conformed to such policy. Such a structure permits the multi-division organization to eliminate the conflict between planning and operating tasks characteristic of a multi-activity firm. In so doing, it extends top management's span of control to encompass the equivalent of several vertically integrated companies.

That economic gains should result from coordinating several multi-activity firms in one administrative hierarchy is not a self-evident proposition. A plausible rationale for giant, multi-division organizations of the sort DuPont and General Motors became in the early 1920's, for instance, is that they enable their component divisions to make particularly efficient use of company-wide expertise in research, marketing, finance, purchasing, and other areas. Indeed, scholars suggest many reasons, although none definitive, to explain why diversified, multi-activity units should perform more efficiently as a group within a multi-division hierarchy than as independent entities in the market [Scherer, 1970, pp. 101-102 and 116-120; Gort, 1966]. Recent empirical evidence further strengthens the idea that entrepreneurs do indeed achieve significant economies by coordinating diverse multi-activity units within multi-division hierarchies [Armour and Teece, 1978].

In their internal accounting systems, multi-division companies such as DuPont and General Motors especially emphasized return on investment. This emphasis suggests that the founders of those organizations attached great importance to how their new hierarchical structures might achieve economies by overcoming imperfections in existing capital markets [Williamson, 1975, pp. 158-162; 1980, pp. 187]. Capital markets have always had limited access to information with which to evaluate the economic performance of vertically integrated, multi-activity firms. Indeed, it is unlikely that participants in external capital markets would ever obtain concerning a multi-activity firm financial information as detailed as that supplied in the monthly operating reports and budgets which division managers at General Motors have submitted to top management since the 1920's. In the past generation, countless multi-division companies have emulated GM's reporting system. The availability of elaborate accounting information enables profit-minded top managers to scrutinize promptly and comprehensively the performance of a division manager within a multi-division company. The performance of the chief executive in an independent, multi-activity firm, however, is evaluated infrequently and imperfectly by outsiders: participants in capital or product markets, stockholders, "raiders," and so forth. Incomplete information prevents these outsiders from making an informed and prompt evaluation of the chief executive's accomplishments. Consequently the situation of the multi-activity firm may become egregious before its case is diagnosed. Slack, inefficient, and opportunistic behavior are difficult to curtail when appraisal of a chief executive's handling of affairs is uninformed [Johnson, 1978, p. 515].

97

The superior performance of divisions does not result entirely from the financial information delivered to top management. There is an even stronger reason that a multi-division firm is able to earn higher profits than could be realized by its combined divisions acting independently. Liberated by subordinates from partisan demands that often compel chief operating managers to accept sub-optimal results, top managers can advocate unqualified pursuit of profit goals set by the capital market. This ability to do so intensifies the pressure on division managers to pursue profit-oriented goals set by top management. It also increases the likelihood that top management will allocate new capital investment among divisions entirely on the basis of the demonstrated capacity of each division to meet the capital market's profit test [Williamson, 1971, pp. 358-359; Johnson, 1978, p. 512]. The historical record leaves no doubt that top management emphasized return on investment in the management accounting system designed for General Motors in the early 1920's because the firm's executives believed that the primary responsibility of top management was to insure that the company earned the required market return on invested capital (the "economic cost of additional capital" according to Donaldson Brown [1924, p. 197]). "The primary object of the corporation," as Alfred P. Sloan [1963, p. 64] insisted, "was to make money, not just to make motor cars."

Another feature of the unique management accounting system designed by General Motors particularly reinforces the notion that the multi-division structure is justified partly by its capacity to coordinate capital transactions more efficiently than can the market system. Its efficient coordination results from the comprehensive use of ex ante information in both forecasts and flexible budgets. Long before the first multi-division companies appeared after World War I, management authorities had advocated that accountants use information about future expectations, as in standard cost accounting, to evaluate current operating results [Chatfield, 1974, pp. 169-171; Wren,

1979, p. 183]. Before the 1920's, however, the idea of controlling operations with proactive rather than reactive financial information did not extend beyond standard cost systems in manufacturing plants.[1] A unique development at General Motors was to place at the very core of its accounting control system forecast information about expected future events [Johnson, 1978]. Through an elaborate forecasting procedure (updated monthly) that made extensive use of "normal volume" standards for both operating costs and capital turnover ratios, the management accounting system facilitated the processing by top management of the information needed to evaluate present and future uses of capital. Moreover, by focusing primarily on the operating and turnover variables that affect return on investment, the monthly divisional operating reports actually reduced the amount of information which top management needed to exercise control.

The multi-division structure, by separating the management tasks in planning from those in operations, certainly makes the best of management's bounded rationality while reducing the possibilities for opportunism implicit in large hierarchies.[2] Indispensable to the smooth functioning of the two specialized management groups in a multi-division firm, however, is an effective internal accounting system. The internal accounting system which executives developed in the 1920's for General Motors refines certain procedures that enable an administrative hierarchy to monitor and allocate the use of capital among diverse products (or industries) and among widely separated geographic regions. By helping management both to increase the efficiency of capital in use and to reduce the amount of capital required to operate, this accounting information surely enables managers of an administrative hierarchy to employ capital more efficiently than would the market system. Given this achievement, management accounting has helped the multi-division structure become, as one economist has called it, "American capitalism's most important single innovation of the 20th century" [Williamson, 1970, p. 175].

IV. Conclusion

Between 1800 and 1930, entrepreneurs in the United States created ingenious internal accounting information systems designed to control the costs of organizing complex economic activities within large-scale, administrative hierarchies. Such systems were essential to a firm's success: over long periods, changes in the information available to economic decision-makers profoundly affected the relative costs of conducting economic activity in markets and hierarchies. And differential changes in those costs at the margin, as Coase [1937] has observed, shift the equilibrium of economic activity between markets and hierarchies. The new management accounting procedures, primarily by mitigating control loss and sub-goal pursuits, enabled many large administrative hierarchies to coordinate complex economic activities more efficiently than could existing market institutions. Developments in management accounting thereby contributed to the shift in nineteenth- and early twentieth-century America toward hierarchical coordination of economic activity in general, and to the growth of large business firms in particular.

---

[1] At DuPont before World War I, forecasting information was used primarily to plan financing, not to control operations [Johnson, 1978, p. 501, n. 20].

[2] One former General Motors executive's view of what happens in a multi-divisional firm when top management becomes involved in operations is portrayed vividly by Wright [1979].

The growth of "big business" in nineteenth- and twentieth-century America was not inevitable, however. Nor must "big business" necessarily continue to exist. Clearly the growth of giant enterprise owes much, as we have seen, to the ingenuity of particular executives. Their innovative management accounting procedures and organizational structures have enabled many large firms to avoid inefficiency and market abuse. Some authorities, however, believe that large-scale hierarchy invites chaos. This claim is certainly not unreasonable. Many giant business organizations in the United States have failed to manage their activities as effectively as they could be managed by either the market or other competing firms. Many giant enterprises have collapsed altogether, and many, despite their inefficiency, carry on because of contrived market imperfections caused by such measures as tariffs, subsidies, and rate regulation. While the falliblity of large-scale enterprises is obvious, equally evident is the increasing power of the market. During the past twenty years, improved technology in communications and in data processing have enormously improved the efficiency of markets, especially capital markets. If the amount of financial information which companies disclose to those markets continues to grow in the future as it has in the last two decades, it is conceivable that future markets will conduct a larger share of the economic activities now being administered by giant hierarchical organizations. It is not inconceivable that historians in the future may recount how improvements in the information used by efficient capital markets during the late twentieth century caused the virtual disappearance of multi-division business organizations.

99

REFERENCES

Alchian, A. A. and H. Demsetz (1972), "Production, Information Costs, and Economic Organization," American Economic Review (December 1972), pp. 777-795.

Amey, L. R. and D. A. Egginton (1973), Management Accounting: A Conceptual Approach (Longman, 1973).

Armour, H. A. and D. J. Teece (1978), "Organizational Structure and Economic Performance: A Test of the Multidivisional Hypothesis," Bell Journal of Economics (Spring, 1978), pp. 106-122.

Arrow, K. J. (1964), "Control in Large Organizations," Management Science (April, 1964), pp. 397-408.

Brief, R. P. (1965), "Nineteenth Century Accounting Error," Journal of Accounting Research (Spring, 1965), pp. 12-31.

Brown, D. (1924), "Pricing Policy in Relation to Financial Control," Management and Administration (February, 1924), pp. 195-198.

Caves, R. E. (1980), "Industrial Organization, Corporate Strategy and Structure," Journal of Economic Literature (March, 1980), pp. 64-92.

Chandler, A. D., Jr. (1966), Strategy and Structure: Chapters in the History of the Industrial Enterprise (Doubleday, 1966).

————————— (1977), The Visible Hand: The Managerial Revolution in American Business (Harvard University Press, 1977).

————————— and F. Redlich (1961), "Recent Developments in American Business Administration and Their Conceptualization," Business History Review (Spring, 1961), pp. 1-31.

————————— and H. Daems (1979), "Administrative Coordination, Allocation and Monitoring: Concepts and Comparisons," in N. Horn and J. Kocka, eds., Law and the Formation of the Big Enterprise in the 19th and Early 20th Centuries (Vanderhoeck and Ruprecht, 1979), pp. 28-52.

Chapman, S. D. (1974), "The Textile Factory Before Arkwright: A Typology of Factory Development," Business History Review (Winter, 1974), pp. 469-473.

Chatfield, M. (1974), A History of Accounting Thought (The Dryden Press, 1974).

Clague, C. (1977), "Information Costs, Corporate Hierarchies, and Earnings Inequality," American Economic Review (February, 1977), pp. 81-85.

Coase, R. (1937), "The Nature of the Firm," Economica (November, 1937), pp. 386-405.

Cooper, W. W. (1951), "A Proposal for Extending the Theory of the Firm," Quarterly Journal of Economics (February, 1951), pp. 87-109.

100

Davis, T. C. (1950), "How the DuPont Organization Appraises Its Performance," American Management Association Financial Management Series No. 94 (1950), pp. 3-7.

Galbraith, J. R. (1972), "Organization Design: An Information Processing View," in J. W. Lorsch and P. R. Lawrence, eds., Organization Planning: Cases and Concepts (Richard D. Irwin, Inc., 1972), pp. 49-74.

Gort, M. (1966), "Diversification, Mergers, and Profit," in W. W. Alberts and J. E. Segall,eds., The Corporate Merger (University of Chicago Press, 1966), ch. 2.

Jelinek, M. (1980), "Toward Systematic Management: Alexander Hamilton Church," Business History Review (Spring, 1980), pp. 63-79.

Johnson, H. T. (1972), "Early Cost Accounting for Internal Management Control: Lyman Mills in the 1850's," Business History Review (Winter, 1972), pp. 466-474.

———————————— (1975), "Management Accounting in an Early Integrated Industrial: E. I. duPont de Nemours Powder Company, 1903-1912," Business History Review (Summer, 1975),pp. 184-204.

———————————— (1978), "Management Accounting in an Early Multidivisional Organization: General Motors in the 1920's," Business History Review (Winter, 1978), pp. 490-517.

Lawrence, P. R. and J. W. Lorsch (1969), Organization and Environment: Managing Differentiation and Integration (Richard D. Irwin, Inc., 1969).

Leibenstein, H. (1979), "A Branch of Economics is Missing: Micro-Micro Theory," Journal of Economic Literature (June, 1979), pp. 477-502.

Litterer, J. A. (1963), "Systematic Management: Design for Organizational Recoupling in American Manufacturing Firms," Business History Review (Winter, 1963), pp. 369-391.

Littleton, A. C. (1933), Accounting Evolution to 1900 (American Institute Publishing Co., 1933).

Marris, R. and D. C. Mueller (1980), "The Corporation, Competition, and the Invisible Hand," Journal of Economic Literature (March, 1980), pp. 32-63.

Porter, D. M. (1980), "The Waltham System and Early American Textile Cost Accounting, 1813-1848," The Accounting Historians Journal (Spring, 1980), pp. 1-15.

Porter, G. (1973), The Rise of Big Business, 1860-1910 (Thomas Y. Crowell Company, 1973).

Scherer, F. M. (1970), Industrial Market Structure and Economic Performance (Rand McNally and Company, 1970).

Simon, H. A. (1979), "Rational Decision Making in Business Organizations," American Economic Review (September, 1979), pp. 493-513.

101

Sloan, A. P., Jr. (1963), My Years With General Motors (Doubleday and Company, Inc., 1963).

Spicer, B. H. and V. Ballew (1980), "Management Accounting Systems and the Economics of Internal Organization," unpublished manuscript, University of Oregon (April, 1980).

Stone, W. E. (1973), "An Early English Cotton Mill Cost Accounting System: Charlton Mills, 1810-1889," Accounting and Business Research (Winter, 1973), pp. 71-78.

Williamson, O. E. (1970), Corporate Control and Business Behavior: An Inquiry Into the Effects of Organization Form on Enterprise Behavior (Prentice-Hall, Inc., 1970).

————————— (1971), "Managerial Discretion, Organization Form, and the Multi-division Hypothesis," in R. Marris and A. Wood, eds., The Corporate Economy: Growth, Competition, and Innovative Potential (Harvard University Press, 1971), pp. 343-386.

————————— (1973), "Markets and Hierarchies: Some Elementary Considerations," American Economic Review (May, 1973), pp. 316-325.

————————— (1975), Markets and Hierarchies: Analysis and Antitrust Implications (The Free Press, 1975).

————————— (1980), "Emergence of the Visible Hand: Implications for Industrial Organization," in A. D. Chandler, Jr. and H. Daems, eds., Managerial Hierarchies: Comparative Perspectives on the Rise of the Modern Industrial Enterprise (Harvard Univ. Press, 1980), pp. 182-202.

Wren, D. A. (1979), The Evolution of Management Thought (John Wiley and Sons, 1979).

Wright, J. P. (1979), On a Clear Day You Can See General Motors: John Z. De Lorean's Look Inside the Automotive Giant (Wright Enterprises, 1979).

102

THE ACCOUNTING REVIEW
Vol. LVI, No. 3
July 1981

Toward a New Understanding of Nineteenth-Century Cost Accounting

H. Thomas Johnson

ABSTRACT: While accounting historians agree that cost accounting is a consequence of the industrial revolution, they have not thoroughly explained the economic consequence of the industrial revolution which prompted manufacturing firms to develop actual cost accounting techniques in the nineteenth century. This paper presents an explanation for the rise of nineteenth-century cost accounting which supplements the traditional view that increased use of fixed capital and the resultant need to account for costs of long-lived assets prompted industrial accountants to graft cost accounts onto the double-entry system. The study concludes that not only changes in the temporal structure of their costs, but also changes in the way they organized economic activity, explain the conditions which prompted manufacturers to develop cost accounting procedures for gathering financial information needed by managers.

104

I. INTRODUCTION

ACCOUNTING historians have long endorsed the view that cost accounting is a product of the industrial revolution. Fifty years ago, Littleton explained that "cost accounting . . . is one of the many consequences of the industrial revolution" [1933, p. 321]. Writing 20 years after Littleton, Garner reinforced this claim when he pointed out that while many industrial bookkeeping procedures existed long before 1800, cost accounting came into existence only after the late eighteenth century [1954, ch. 1].

In addition to agreeing about when cost accounting was developed, accounting historians have long shared a particular view of why cost accounting arose when it did. This traditional view contends that the increased use of fixed capital prompted accountants during the industrial revolution to graft cost ac-counting onto the double-entry system. For example, Garner states that the "relative simplicity" of late eighteenth-century accounting in engineering, coal mining, and textile firms did not suffice after 1800 when "problems arose mainly in connection with the large amounts of capital sunk in plant equipment and transportation facilities" [1954, p. 28].

The author gratefully acknowledges the comments received from Charles T. Horngren, Elaine B. Johnson, Robert J. Lord, and three anonymous reviewers for this journal. Earlier versions of this paper were presented to the 1979 Washington Community College Accounting Workshop and to the 1980 Western Regional Conference of the American Accounting Association.

H. Thomas Johnson is Professor of Accounting, Western Washington University.

Manuscript received May 1980.
Revision received August 1980.
Accepted October 1980.

More recently, furthermore, Chatfield observes that "the main new fact confronting both financial and cost accountants" at the beginning of the industrial era "was the presence of large amounts of capital sunk in plant and equipment" [1974, p. 101].

This widely held belief, so ably expressed by Chatfield and Garner, does not seem to me to explain fully the conditions responsible for the rise of cost accounting. Various recent studies [Johnson, 1972; Stone, 1973; Chandler, 1977; Wells, 1977; Porter, 1980] of how the managers of nineteenth-century manufacturing firms used accounting information to facilitate decision-making and control have resulted in some findings which seem inconsistent with the traditional explanation of why the industrial revolution caused cost accounting to develop. For example, modern studies have revealed that near the beginning of the nineteenth century textile factories relied upon double-entry cost accounting information to control multi-process operations. This was, however, long before fixed assets consumed a manager's attention. Indeed, Chatfield [1974, p. 101] observes that "investing in fixed assets did not seem very different from buying inventories" in the minds of early nineteenth-century industrial managers.[1] These investigations have further indicated that some capital-intensive manufacturing firms near the end of the nineteenth century which used cost accounting information for decision-making and control were not particularly concerned with the problem of allocating fixed costs to periods or to products.

The pioneering work done in these studies suggests that the demand for procedures with which to account for fixed capital does not explain fully why cost accounting actually emerged when it did. The following analysis offers the view that new methods for organizing economic activity—not just changes in the temporal structure of their costs—explain why many nineteenth-century industrial organizations developed cost-accounting procedures. Nineteenth-century industrial firms were among the first in history to use internal administrative procedures to coordinate multiple processes involving the conversion of raw materials into finished goods. Although these firms often invested in fixed plant and equipment, their concern for internal cost accounting information was dictated not only by the need to account for fixed costs, but also by the need to evaluate and control internally-administered production processes.

II. The Origin of Cost Accounting in Nineteenth-Century Textile Factories

The first modern business organizations to require internal accounting information for decision-making and control were the mechanized, multi-process, cotton textile factories that appeared in England and the United States around 1800. These textile factories used cost accounts to ascertain the direct labor and overhead costs of converting raw material into finished yarn and fabric. These double-entry cost accounts, so far the earliest discovered, differ radically from any accounting records used previously

105

---

[1] Chatfield's observation is supported by the limited empirical evidence on asset structures of early factories which economic historians frequently cite. For example, Mathias [1969, p. 148], referring to conditions in late eighteenth- and early nineteenth-century Britain, states that "even in the early factories, in textiles, breweries and the like, amongst the most heavily capitalized less than one-seventh or one-eighth of total assets typically were in buildings and plant; six-sevenths to seven-eights and more still being absorbed by 'movables' or 'circulating capital'...." Chandler [1977, p. 71], referring to early nineteenth-century American textile manufacturers, notes that "as labor and cotton were by far the major costs, they had little incentive to compute indirect and overhead costs."

in business organizations. From the inception of double-entry bookkeeping until the advent of the modern factory, businesses had used accounts merely to record the results of market exchanges. With the arrival of the integrated, multi-process textile mill, however, accounts were needed to synthesize information about the cost of internal, administratively coordinated production activities.[2] In 1931, D. R. Scott noted the consequence of factory developments for accounting in *The Cultural Significance of Accounts*:

> Before the industrial revolution, accounting was mainly a record of the external relations of one business unit with other business units, a record of relations determined in the market. But with the advent of large scale productive operations . . . necessity arose for more emphasis upon the accounting for interests within the competitive unit and upon the use of accounting records as a means of administrative control over the enterprise. . . . The appearance of cost accounts in manufacturing . . . is [an] example [Scott, 1931, p. 143].

When it introduced a new mode of organizing production, the modern factory necessitated the development of a new kind of accounting activity.

To understand why the early textile factory's unique system of production required a new type of accounting information, consider the information required by merchants in the so-called "domestic" system, a market system that preceded the appearance of modern textile factories, pervaded economically developed areas of Europe and North America, and coordinated textile production as well as many other types of production [Pollard, 1965, p. 214; Holderness, 1976, pp. 107–109; Wells, 1978, pp. 41, 44 and 46]. In general, the domestic system consisted of merchants and artisans who coordinated the transformation of raw materials into finished goods through autonomous market exchanges.

Specifically, a merchant-entrepreneur bought raw materials such as cotton, silk, or wool in open markets and consigned these materials to independent household artisans (i.e., "domestic" artisans). Using equipment they owned or rented, the artisans transformed the raw goods into finished yarn or fabric. A merchant compensated an artisan according to market-determined piece-rates, and he sold the finished goods in open markets. Although the merchant kept accounts to record past exchanges and to keep track of widely scattered inventories, obviously he did not need those accounts to provide information for decision-making and and control.[3] Market prices supplied all the managerial information he needed: namely, prices for finished goods and prices for all the inputs going into his cost of production. Input prices encompassed purchase prices of raw materials, market piece-rates paid to artisans, and market prices paid for inputs other than raw materials and labor.

Market prices no longer supplied all the information needed for decision-making and control once merchant-entrepreneurs administered the coordination of textile-making processes in centralized work places.[4] In the domestic system, information about labor and

---

[2] Loveday [1980] shows how managers used cost accounting information to coordinate multi-process mills in the cut nail industry around 1870.

[3] The Medici accounts, housed in the Baker Library at Harvard Business School, show how a pre-industrial domestic organization could maintain excellent accounts of external financial transactions and of physical inventories but not require, apparently, cost *per se*. For a succinct discussion of the Medici accounts see Garner [1954, pp. 7–15].

[4] In early proto-factories, such as Adam Smith's famous pin factory, multiple processes could be centralized without being coordinated administratively [Chapman, 1974]. Such organizations did not require cost records if all inputs, including labor, were paid at market prices for output produced. Cost records became essential only after administrators assumed the task of coordinating the conversion of inputs into output.

overhead conversion costs had been automatically supplied to merchants by market prices. In the factory, because wage contracts between employer and employee were substituted for market piece-rate contracts between merchant and artisan, and because nonlabor conversion inputs were often supplied internally, managers found it necessary to *account for* internal conversion costs. The market wage they paid to workers, for instance, contained only part of the information which managers needed to ascertain labor conversion cost. The missing part of the information was, of course, the worker's productivity during the time he earned his wage. Whereas piece-rates that automatically matched money and output supplied the labor portion of conversion costs in the market-mediated domestic system, special *accounts* that matched internally coordinated flows of money and output were required to synthesize these labor conversion costs in the administratively organized factory system. By making it necessary to account for both labor and other conversion costs, administrative coordination of multiple processes in early textile factories thereby imposed internal cost accounting upon double-entry bookkeeping.

The earliest factory cost records so far known to historians are from integrated, multi-process textile mills. This is true, for instance, of the Charlton Mills in England around 1800 [Stone, 1973]; it applies to the Boston Manufacturing Company by the 1820s [Porter, 1980];[5] and it is true of the Lyman Mills Company around 1850 [Johnson, 1972]. The cost records in these firms indicate the labor portion of the conversion cost at each stage of a textile mill's production cycle. Generally, these records include both registers showing the daily or weekly wages paid to workers and also log books

recording the pounds of cotton converted each day in processes such as picking, carding, roving, spinning, warping and weaving, and dyeing and finishing. By combining data from these two sets of records, it is possible to determine the direct labor cost per unit of output by process at least daily, although most firms seem to have reported this information once a month. Sometimes, moreover, these mills gathered periodic information about more than the direct cost per unit of output for labor. For instance, they acquired information by process about direct cost per unit of output for overhead items such as repairs, maintenance, bleach, dyes, fuel, and teaming.

It should be noted that the cost reports just described were certainly an integral part of the double-entry records [cf. Garner, 1954, ch. 6; Previts and Merino, 1979, pp. 62–74]. Data on wages and other conversion expenses came from the general accounts used to record the payment of liabilities. Furthermore, data on departmental flows of raw material quantities were reconciled with physical inventory counts every six months. Although these early textile mills did not often keep perpetual inventory records as such, they did keep track of the weight of cotton flowing in and out of departments, and they kept an elaborate account of cotton bales on order and received.

The managers of early textile mills used information from these nascent cost records to make short-run decisions and to achieve control in the one aspect of their operation not governed by market exchange prices: namely, the conversion of raw materials into finished goods.

[5] Volumes 80, 84, and 90 of the Boston Manufacturing Co. Payroll Records, filed in Baker Library at Harvard University, indicate a shift from piece-rate to wage payment around 1821.

Competitive market prices beyond the manager's control dictated, of course, the exchange rates for finished goods, for raw materials, supplies, and the laborers' time. The mill manager himself, however, could influence the rate at which laborers, using other inputs, converted raw cotton into yarn or fabric. Information from accounts about the cost of that conversion activity aided the manager's task of evaluation and control. Such information included the conversion cost per pound of output by department for each worker and for each type of direct overhead expense. Moreover, correspondence between mill foremen and marketing officials in early cotton textile companies indicates that they made short-run decisions about special-order prices and equipment modifications using contribution margin information that was derived from these direct conversion costs [Johnson, 1972, p. 474].

Besides giving management short-run decision and control information, these first cost accounts also provided incentives and controls that prevented employee opportunism from dissipating the productivity gains inherent in mechanized, multi-process systems. Workers had a natural inclination, of course, to use their time efficiently when paid piecerates; they had no automatic incentive to pursue the same goal when being paid a wage. Managers of early textile mills could monitor employee performance with periodic cost information that compared productivity among workers in the same process at a specific time and that also compared productivity for one or more workers over several periods of time [Chandler, 1977, p. 69]. The capacity of managerial accounts such as these, then, to promote goal congruence in a hierarchical system and to provide cost information about internally-coordinated processes clearly indicates that

industrial organizations used double-entry systems to gather useful managerial cost information long before they used such systems to account for the costs of long-lived assets.

III. COST ACCOUNTING IN LATE NINE-TEENTH-CENTURY, CAPITAL-INTENSIVE MANUFACTURING FIRMS

Capital-intensive manufacturing operations conducted by the late 1800s in iron and steel, foodstuffs, petroleum, chemicals, machinery-making, and so forth, were vastly more complex and larger than were operations within the early nineteenth-century New England textile industry. Nevertheless, at the end of the century most of these large manufacturing organizations still conducted, as had the early textile firms, only one basic activity: namely, the conversion of raw materials into finished goods [Chandler, 1977, ch. 8]. It is plausible, therefore, that refined and elaborate versions of the conversion cost systems which originated in early textile factories also supplied the management accounting information used to control operating activities in the giant descendants of the first textile mills. And it is also possible that these capital-intensive giants gave greater attention than did early textile firms to the problem of allocating fixed costs to periods or to products. Much research needs to be done before we can say definitely how managers of these giant organizations used accounting information to administer capital-intensive manufacturing activities during the late 1800s. Although accounting historians have assiduously studied writings by late nineteenth-century authorities on cost accounting, they have virtually ignored the managerial accounting information actually used in late nineteenth-century capital-intensive manufacturing firms.

A glimpse into the use of management

accounts by late nineteenth-century, capital-intensive manufacturers is provided in the accounting information used by one of the shrewdest entrepreneurs of that era, Andrew Carnegie. Historians [Krooss and Gilbert, 1972, p. 207] have observed that Carnegie made a fetish of using cost statements to manage his giant steel company from 1872 to 1902. It seems surprising, therefore, that accounting historians have not described or analyzed Carnegie's particular cost accounting system. From brief descriptions provided by Carnegie, by his biographers, and by other historians, one concludes that his system was not designed to account for fixed costs of long-lived assets [Wall, 1970, pp. 325–349, 504–506, and 583–586; Livesay, 1975, *passim*; Chandler, 1977, pp. 267–268]. What it did feature was a continuous gathering of data on all direct costs in every process of the manufacturing activity, from blast furnace to rolling mill. With weekly data on direct material and conversion costs for each process in his mills, Carnegie apparently had all the accounting information he required in order to invest more capital and to earn higher returns than any other steelmaker in the world before 1902.

The only other financial information which Carnegie seems to have relied upon to make both operating decisions and investment decisions was informa-about his competitors' direct production costs. Carnegie's operating strategy was to push his own direct costs below those of all competitors so that he could charge prices that would always ensure enough demand to keep his plants running at full capacity. He therefore needed, and got, frequent information showing his direct costs in relation to those of his competitors. With that information in hand, and secure in the knowledge that his costs were the lowest in the industry,

Carnegie then engaged in merciless price-cutting during economic recessions. While competing firms went under, he still made profits. In periods of prosperity, when customers' demands exceeded the industry's capacity to produce, Carnegie then joined others in raising prices.

The information he had on his own and his competitors' direct material and conversion costs also enabled Carnegie to make rational investment decisions. The basic rule governing his investment decisions was to invest in new steel-making capacity whenever a new process appeared that offered lower direct costs than did his present processes. In order to keep informed about the latest steel technology, Carnegie and his corps of highly trained experts travelled extensively in Europe and the United States. When he decided, then, that a new investment embodied the lowest-cost technology available, it was an informed decision. Moreover, his apparent reliance on nothing more than differential direct costs to evaluate long-term capital investment decisions was rational if one assumes that Carnegie believed the long-run demand for his product at his price to be essentially infinite. Carnegie's always bullish marketing attitude suggests that he never thought otherwise.

Carnegie's example certainly demonstrates that accounting easily kept pace with the information needs of managers in large single-activity manufacturing concerns during the late 1800s. Historians observe that accounting records used by managers of those capital-intensive giants often gave inadequate attention either to asset depreciation [Brief, 1965, pp. 21–30] or to full-absorption product costing [Chatfield, 1974, pp. 102 and 160]. Nor did nineteenth-century industrialists develop the forecasts or the return-on-investment data that one might expect a capital-intensive firm would need

[Johnson, 1975, pp. 448–449]. Apparently, these single-activity organizations, operating in the expansive market environment of late nineteenth-century America, did not absolutely require accounting information to select and plan investments. As Carnegie's case demonstrates, success often depended upon good information about direct operating costs. For that, accounting systems mattered. For the rest, faith and intuition sufficed.

IV. CONCLUSION

The records both of early nineteenth-century textile mills and of giant manufacturing firms operating later in the century do not support the traditional hypothesis that the increased use of fixed assets prompted the development of industrial cost accounting. Instead, the evidence seems to support the conclusion that changes in the way they organized economic activity, not just changes in the temporal structure of their costs, prompted nineteenth-century industrial organizations to develop internal cost accounting procedures.

The definition of cost accounting used by most accounting historians "is normally reserved for integrated cost and financial accounting systems which involve the allocation of indirect and fixed expenses" [Wells, 1977, p. 47].[6] The definition used in this paper is the equivalent of "direct costing," designed to provide financial information for management decision-making and control. Although most historians clearly distinguish between managerial and financial uses of accounting information, their commentaries on nineteenth-century cost accounting practices show a distinct bias toward those developments which foreshadowed the twentieth-century concern for matching costs with realized revenue and for attaching manu-

facturing costs to products [cf. Hudson, 1977, p. 17]. This bias is evident in the concern which accounting historians show for: the integration of cost and financial accounts [Littleton, 1933, ch. 21; Garner, 1954, ch. 6; Chatfield, 1974, pp. 104–105, 159–160, and 162–163]; methods to cost inventories of goods finished and in process [Littleton, 1933, pp. 337–339; Garner, 1954, ch. 10; Chatfield, 1971, p. 11]; procedures to assign *full* costs of production to manufactured products [Littleton, 1933, ch. 21; Chatfield, 1971, p. 12].

The bias toward twentieth-century financial reporting concepts of cost accounting is also implicit in the contention of accounting historians that "true" double-entry cost accounting did not appear until very late in the nineteenth century, when accounting authorities first wrote about integrated systems for costing products. Ironically, many of those authorities who wrote about product costing from 1885 to 1914 were interested not in accounting, but rather in estimating [Wells, 1978]. They were writing as engineers interested in devising rational, uniform systems for pricing unique products in non-competitive markets. For this reason, they paid attention to the problems of how to allocate fixed costs to products in manufacturing enterprises. They had no fundamental interest in accounting *per se*.

The evidence now available in company records suggests that manufacturing organizations used modern financial accounting procedures to account for the costs of fixed assets only after the turn of the twentieth century [Johnson, 1975,

---

[6] Although Littleton differentiated the prime cost accounting information that early factories needed from the cost allocation information that later capital-intensive establishments needed, he reserved the title "cost accounting" exclusively for the latter activity [Littleton, 1933, p. 322, last paragraph].

110

pp. 448–449]) Historians have not ascertained which businesses first used these full cost procedures for financial reporting purposes, nor have they explained what prompted the widespread adoption of such procedures after 1900. On closer study of actual company records, historians may discover that legal reporting requirements, such as those embodied in income tax statutes or in government contract regulations, caused the wide diffusion of financial accounting procedures for product costing.

The notion explored in this paper—that the nonmarket coordination of economic activity necessitates the development of managerial cost accounting—can be used to explain more than just the development of internal cost accounting practices in nineteenth-century manufacturing firms. By comparing how various societies organize economic activity, historians may also gain valuable insight into nineteenth- and twentieth-century differences in cost accounting practice among nations [cf. Wells, 1977, p. 52]. Nineteenth-century English writers, for instance, frequently remarked that England's textile industry paid less attention to cost accounting than did America's textile industry [Locke, 1979]. If that observation is correct, then historians attempting to explain the reasons for American "superiority" might profitably search for differences in the way in which textile production was organized in the two countries. Perhaps historians eventually will trace the difference between English and American accounting procedures to the fact that American mills tended to be integrated, multi-process operations, whereas English mills, often much larger in size, tended to specialize in single processes [Mathias, 1969, p. 266]. Companies that specialize in one mechanical process do not need accounting records to ascertain their costs; companies which integrate two or more processes in a continuous flow cannot know their costs without such records. The so-called "failure" of nineteenth-century English textile companies to adopt what are often considered as advanced American cost accounting procedures may have been a consequence of the effectiveness of market institutions in England. This very effectiveness would have made it beneficial for English mills to coordinate different production processes by means of market exchange. Effective market institutions, by eliminating the economic advantages of administratively coordinating different production processes, made sophisticated internal cost accounting procedures unnecessary.

111

REFERENCES

Brief, R. P. (1965), "Nineteenth Century Accounting Error," *Journal of Accounting Research* (Spring, 1965), pp. 12–31.

Chandler, A. D., Jr. (1977), *The Visible Hand: The Managerial Revolution in American Business* (Harvard University Press, 1977).

Chapman, S. D. (1974), "The Textile Factory Before Arkwright: A Typology of Factory Development," *Business History Review* (Winter, 1974), pp. 451–478.

Chatfield, M. (1971), "The Origins of Cost Accounting," *Management Accounting* (June 1971), pp. 11–14.

——— (1974), *A History of Accounting Thought* (The Dryden Press, 1974).

Garner, S. P. (1954), *Evolution of Cost Accounting to 1925* (University of Alabama Press, 1954).

Holderness, B. A. (1976), *Pre-Industrial England: Economy and Society, 1500 to 1750* (J. M. Dent and Sons, Ltd., 1976).

Hudson, P. (1977), "Some Aspects of 19th Century Accounting Development in the West Riding Textile Industry," *Accounting History* (November 1977), pp. 4–22.

Johnson, H. T. (1972), "Early Cost Accounting for Internal Management Control: Lyman Mills in the 1850's," *Business History Review* (Winter, 1972), pp. 466–474.

—— (1975), "The Role of Accounting History in the Study of Modern Business Enterprise," THE ACCOUNTING REVIEW (July 1975), pp. 444–450.

Krooss, H. E., and C. Gilbert (1972), *American Business History* (Prentice-Hall, 1972).

Littleton, A. C. (1933), *Accounting Evolution to 1900* (American Institute Publishing Co., 1933).

Livesay, H. C. (1975), *Andrew Carnegie and the Rise of Big Business* (Little, Brown, and Company, 1975).

Locke, R. R. (1979), "Cost Accounting: An Institutional Yardstick for Measuring British Entrepreneurial Performance, circa 1914," *The Accounting Historians Journal* (Fall, 1979), pp. 1–22.

Loveday, A. J. (1980), "Technology, Cost Accounting, and Management in the Cut Nail Industry of the Upper Ohio Valley, 1865–1890," in P. J. Uselding, ed., *Business and Economic History* (University of Illinois, 1980), pp. 41–50.

Mathias, P. (1969), *The First Industrial Nation: An Economic History of Britain, 1700–1914* (Methuen & Co., Ltd., 1969).

Pollard, S., (1965), *The Genesis of Modern Management* (Harvard University Press, 1965).

Porter, D. M. (1980), "The Waltham System and Early American Textile Cost Accounting, 1813–1848," *The Accounting Historians Journal* (Spring, 1980), pp. 1–15.

Previts, G. J., and B. D. Merino (1979), *A History of Accounting in America* (The Ronald Press, 1979).

Scott, D R (1931), *The Cultural Significance of Accounts* (Henry Holt and Company, 1931).

Stone, W. E. (1973), "An Early English Cotton Mill Cost Accounting System: Charlton Mills, 1810–1889," *Accounting and Business Research* (Winter, 1973), pp. 71–78.

Wall, J. F. (1970), *Andrew Carnegie* (Oxford University Press, 1970).

Wells, M. C. (1977), "Some Influences on the Development of Cost Accounting," *The Accounting Historians Journal* (Fall 1977), pp. 47–61.

—— (1978), *Accounting for Common Costs* (University of Illinois Center for International Research in Accounting, 1978).

112

Accounting, Organizations and Society, Vol. 8, No. 2/3, pp. 139—146, 1983.
Printed in Great Britain.

0361—3682/83 $3.00 + .00
Pergamon Press Ltd.

THE SEARCH FOR GAIN IN MARKETS AND FIRMS: A REVIEW OF THE HISTORICAL EMERGENCE OF MANAGEMENT ACCOUNTING SYSTEMS*

H. THOMAS JOHNSON

University of Puget Sound
Tacoma, WA 98416, U.S.A.

Abstract

This essay explores the organizational conditions underlying the emergence and role of management accounting and the organizational processes through which management accounting affects society. Management accounting emerged to provide information needed by organizers of firms—economic entities that operate partly outside of the market system. Organizers create firms in order to earn higher returns from economic resources than they can earn through ordinary market exchange. Management accounting information defines the internally-controlled domain of opportunities in which organizers search for higher returns. This information also influences the effort that organizers and other members of a firm make to derive gains from internally-controlled resources; and it shapes the opinion that society holds of firms' activities.

113

A. Bogdanov stated that:

Existence of social classes is due not to the distribution of ownership rights in society but arises because of the possession of organizational experience by individuals in a given society. Thus, the ruling class in a social system is composed of organizers of production and not the owners of the means of production. The elimination of class distinction in society, therefore, cannot be achieved through violent revolutions and abolition of private ownership rights, but rather through education of members of society in organizational skills (quoted in Gorelik, 1975, p. 12).

Scholars who regard accounting as a social and organizational phenomenon would surely appreciate that the history of management accounting is part of the history of the firm and that the history of double-entry bookkeeping is part of the history of the market system. Accounting historians, however, seldom explore the organizational conditions underlying the emergence and role of accounting. Nor do they examine the organizational processes through which accounting affects society. Instead, they seem to believe "that accounting systems are . . . 'independent' variables, standing in organizational isolation" (Hopwood, 1977, p. 188). In so doing, they imply that accounting develops according to some internal dynamic inherent in the double-entry process.[1]

Methods of management accounting, however, which have been routinely used in the United States and England since the late eighteenth century, actually emerged to serve organizational

---

* I want to thank Anthony Hopwood and Elaine B. Johnson for helpful suggestions and editorial refinements, without implicating either of them in the errors, omissions and inconsistencies that remain.

[1] In tracing the history of cost accounting, for example, historians argue that modern product costing developed as it did because it fulfilled an inherent need to integrate cost accounts into double-entry financial accounts. See Littleton (1933, chs. 20 and 21), Garner (1954, ch. 6), and Chatfield (1971). For an alternative view that considers how organizational forces created the need for early industrial cost accounting, see Johnson (1981).

structures, themselves ultimately the product of complex human goals. Without industrial cost accounting, budgeting, performance appraisal and other accounting procedures devised to provide financial information, organizations could not conduct economic activity. Indeed, the emphatic demand for management accounting information came from firms: in other words, from economic organizations operating at least in part outside the market system. To understand the impetus that gave rise to management accounting, then, one must consider the historical conditions that led to the creation of firms in the western market economy.

114

THE ORIGIN OF FIRMS IN THE WESTERN MARKET ECONOMY

The market economy, originating among Mediterranean and Baltic societies around 1000 A.D. and spreading throughout Europe and North America by the late eighteenth century, consisted of various institutions for autonomous trade and exchange which permitted people to search freely among all available economic opportunities. Because of the incentive that the institution of private property gave individuals to search for productive opportunities, the market system contributed significantly to the cumulative growth of economic productivity in the western world (North & Thomas, 1970 and 1973).[2] It also encouraged the development of extensive trading networks. It was these networks which necessitated the rise of double-entry bookkeeping. Since early traders and merchants rarely used currency to settle exchange, their transactions often involved elaborate claims and counterclaims. To avoid disputes and to settle transactions unambiguously, traders and merchants devised systems of account-keeping so that they could

remember and, if necessary, enforce claims and debts. Double-entry accounts responded, then, to the needs of the traders and to the peculiarities of their market system. Indeed, prior to the late-eighteenth century, keeping track of what was owing and owed seems to have been the main purpose of double-entry accounts (Baxter, 1979, p. 9).[3] The information needed to conduct economic activity through market exchanges — to search for, and select, economic opportunities — was provided by market prices, not by double-entry accounts.

Eventually, of course, double-entry bookkeeping transformed into modern managerial accounting. This metamorphosis was brought about by the creation of firms: economic organizations, that is to say, operating partly outside the market system. For, with the emergence of firms beginning near the close of the eighteenth century and continuing into our own, certain economic activities came to be conducted within the firm itself, rather than in the market place.

Firms arose when individuals perceived opportunities for personal gain greater than those offered through ordinary market exchange. The particular opportunity that probably catalyzed the appearance of business firms was an increase, during the early eighteenth century, in market demand for textiles in Western Europe (Landes, 1969, pp. 56—60; Marglin, 1976, pp. 28—41; Francis, 1979, pp. 5- 6; Johnson, 1981). If merchant entrepreneurs who provided textiles (produced in the familiar market-coordinated "putting-out" system by myriad self-employed artisans) could increase their supply to meet the heightened demand, then they stood to profit enormously. To increase supply, however, by relying upon the market-coordinated, putting-out system was extremely difficult. Merchants could contract work out to more artisans. But to substantially increase the work force proved costly,

---

[2] The unprecedented growth of productivity since the industrial revolution caused earlier historians to attribute rising living standards in the West to industrialization. Today historians view industrialization as one event (although a uniquely significant one) in a long progression of productivity-raising developments prompted by market search and the incentive of private gain at least since the twelfth century.

[3] Baxter (1979, p. 6), writing of colonial America, suggests that double-entry account-keeping might not have appeared before the industrial era if all transactions of traders had always involved exchange for cash.

inconvenient, and inefficient for it necessitated travelling to supervise more and more laborers; and it also led to diminished control over quality of output. Nor did merchants succeed in enticing each individual worker to produce more by offering him a higher piece-rate. When the early eighteenth-century domestic artisan received a higher price for his output, he often perceived an opportunity to relax and produce less. Seldom did the higher piece-rate motivate him to increase his output. The case offers a classic example of a backward-bending labor supply curve.

To meet the increased market demand for textiles, merchants finally understood that they must eradicate the decentralized putting-out, piece-rate contract which allowed each laborer to decide for himself how productive he would be. They replaced that contract with a centralized "factory" wage contract. In other words, merchants became employers. They gained control over labor productivity by establishing a centralized firm and administering the tasks of wage earners. Consequently, merchants were in a position to compel individual workers to produce more than they would ever turn out under market conditions in a putting-out system.[4] Now merchants could readily increase supplies of textiles to meet growing demands.

EARLY COST ACCOUNTS IN THE FACTORY

Having solved one problem, however, they encountered another. Having assumed control of labor productivity, organizers of the first textile factories discovered that the information required to evaluate labor conversion cost, and which had previously been supplied by market prices in the form of piece-rates, was not provided by the wage contract. Consequently, they devised a means of ingeniously replicating that information: cost

accounting. Double-entry cost accounts provided information about labor and other conversion costs per unit of output for each worker and every process in the factory. This entirely new type of accounting system anticipated modern managerial accounting (Johnson, 1981).

If we assume that the only purpose of these new managerial accounts was to replicate unit conversion cost information that had previously been supplied by market piece-rates, we shall miss their extensive social and economic impact. The information in these accounts actually defined a new domain for the search for gain that was quite unlike the market place. In the earliest markets, the "invisible hand" of market forces controlled the search for gains from increased productivity. In the new domain of the firm, human organizers "visibly" controlled non-market activities (such as the production process, in the case of early textile factories); and they also controlled property rights to any gains from increased productivity.[5] Information from the new cost accounts, therefore, defined a non-market domain for search that was governed by the organizers' self-interest.

Historians have not thoroughly documented the uses that early factory organizers made of the information contained in their cost accounts. It is likely, however, that access to figures on unit conversion costs significantly encouraged factory owners to search persistently for new forms of power and mechanization. Mechanization and fossil-fuel power sources were not necessary, of course, for the shift to take place from market to non-market control over production processes. Once non-market control over production processes had become a reality. however, management accounting information concerning factory conversion costs must surely have inspired factory organizers to seek new ways of raising productivity. Sombart's thesis about the influence of double-entry accounting on capitalist development, while

115

---

[4] An unanswered question is how merchants at first enticed or coerced artisans to become factory wage earners. One theory is that they relied, initially, on the labor of children and young women, relatively powerless groups who may have been coerced by family to work in factories. In time, then, the factory system's higher productivity compelled "inefficient" mature male artisans to join ranks.

[5] Competitive market prices beyond their control could force factory organizers to share these gains, of course, with workers (and other input suppliers) and/or consumers. But this would depend on the market power of those groups.

surely erroneous before 1800, may well be an accurate reflection of accounting's influence on the diffusion of new factory technology during the nineteenth century.

One telling indication that cost accounting significantly motivated factory organizers to search for ways to drive slack out of the production process was the great emphasis placed by members of the scientific management movement between about 1890 to 1914 on standard cost accounting. By the late 1800s, the quest for improved factory production methods was conducted largely by engineers, and these engineers viewed the factory conversion process purely in terms of technical engineering conversion coefficients. Despite their obvious inclination to interpret standards from the point of view of physical engineering, many management engineers still recommended standard *cost* information as the means to monitor production efficiency. Moreover, they often justified their procedure by affirming its ability to combat soldiering or, in other words, to drive slack out of the labor conversion process.

MANAGEMENT ACCOUNTING IN THE VERTICALLY-INTEGRATED FIRM

At the turn of the century, however, a new form of non-market organization appeared. This new form, the vertically-integrated firm, would lead to dramatic changes in management accounting practices. Far less radical were those practices — such as the development of standard costing — which had resulted from the technical concerns of shop-floor engineers in the factory. The vertically integrated firm did not concentrate exclusively on production. Rather, it combined this activity with such activities as marketing, purchasing, and transportation (Williamson, 1975, ch. 5; Chandler, 1977, part IV). These complex combinations enabled organizers of giant, mass-producing manufacturing firms to take advantage of their substantial curtailment of slack in the production activity. Having achieved unprecedented speeds of throughput, mass producers who were engaged in such endeavors as steel making, petroleum refining, farm implement manufacture, and food

processing recognized that their sophisticated production processes were not well served by the ordinary market. Indeed, ordinary market exchange for their finished output, as well as for many of their crucial raw material inputs, prevented them from capturing all the gains that could be realized by means of their effective techniques. Some producers dealing through traditional wholesale networks were reaching fewer customers and selling less output than would surely have been the case were they negotiating directly with the final customer. Although producers could offer inducements to wholesalers in an effort to expand sales, such inducements were risky and often ineffectual. After all, the wholesaler was inevitably less concerned to promote a particular product than was the manufacturer. Furthermore, a manufacturer could not effectively monitor a wholesaler's performance under gain-sharing contracts. Many mass-producers, then, in order to control and streamline the distribution market, found it necessary either to institute or acquire their own retail market activity. To further advance their interests, the mass producers obtained control of raw material inputs, especially in cases where they doubted that raw material suppliers were passing on in the form of lower prices the scale-economies they themselves enjoyed from supplying large orders for giant manufacturers. To capture those gains, the organizers moved the purchasing activity from the market to the firm. By controlling the supply activity, the firm could drive out the slack that existed in the market transaction.

Organizers of vertically integrated firms seized on any opportunity, whether it entailed controlling the supply of raw material or handling final customer demand, to drive slack out of an entire industry. In fact, these creators of non-market organizations took unprecedented advantage of society's resources. It is no surprise, then, that in their quest for personal gain they also developed new management accounting information to serve their task. To be sure, organizers of multi-activity firms continued to rely on the same types of management accounting information — unit conversion costs and sales turnover rates — that single-activity firms had previously used to evaluate and control performance in activities such as manufacturing and retail distribution. That information alone was sufficient for the purposes of single-activity firms where the organizers' search for ways to drive internal or, in other words, non-market, resources was limited to single conversion processes such as production or selling. It was not sufficient, however, in vertically-integrated firms where the effort to profit from the internal management of resources entailed the non-market coordination of multiple activities.

The non-market domain of the vertically-integrated firm required, for instance, the information made available through budgeting. Comprehensive budgets, both for the entire enterprise and for each of its constituent departments, enabled the firm's organizers to coordinate and balance the operating capacities of the separate departments. Furthermore, the information in budgets provided norms which allowed organizers of a vertically integrated firm to periodically evaluate the firm's various activities. This management accounting procedure revealed whether an activity was contributing to higher financial returns for the enterprise as a whole. In this way, budget norms served a purpose similar to that served by standard costs. These norms were not set scientifically, however, and they encompassed a much broader domain than the factory shop floor.

Indeed, so broad was the domain for search for gain in a vertically integrated firm that it necessitated the creation of common financial measurements which permitted evaluating and controlling the disparate activities of the enterprise. One such measurement was cash flow. Cash budgets for planning and control provided information about the contribution that each constituent department made to a firm's total performance. Another common means of measuring the performance of various departments in a massive enterprise was return on investment (ROI). Tremendously important, ROI would in the long run affect management accounting practice more than would cash flow. Once they had obtained information from cash budgets, the firm's organizers used additional information on the amount of capital invested in each distinct activity of the vertically-integrated enterprise. With these data, they could assess ROI throughout the organization.

Although extremely useful procedures, ROI budgets were seldom used for planning and control before the 1920s. Even before World War I, however, the firm that seems to have invented ROI accounting, the DuPont Corporation, had a remarkably sophisticated ROI budgeting system (Johnson, 1975). That budgeting system connected the use of resources, wherever they were employed in the firm, to the organizers' ROI goal. Lying behind the system was Donaldson Brown's formula, familiar today to every undergraduate accounting student, equating ROI to the product of sales turnover and the operating margin. Information from that budgeting system links performance in virtually every one of the firm's activity centers to the organizers' ROI goal.

This budgeting system, an essential part of the managerial accounting system developed by the E.I. DuPont de Nemours Powder Company between 1903 and 1912, is mentioned here not because of its remarkable sophistication. It is important because it defined the domain of the organizers' search for personal gain differently than had any previous management accounting system. Certainly the founders of the DuPont Powder Company did emulate others in creating their vertically-integrated firm in order to drive slack out of retail and raw material markets. They were absolutely unique, however, because they designed a management accounting system intended to assess returns exclusively in relation to capital invested in the business. This emphasis caused them to select ROI to measure the results of the non-market activities under their control. Even more significantly, it also compelled them to attend single-mindedly to wringing out of capital every conceivable advantage.

One obvious way to accomplish this objective was to reduce inefficiencies within giant, vertically-integrated organizations. Understandably, the size and complexity of the large, bureaucratically structured firm inevitably precluded realizing every possible gain conceivably attendant upon the non-market coordination of industry resources. Size and complexity, however, did not prevent curtailing organizational slack. Given sufficient incentive, those controlling a firm's internal affairs could always streamline operations. For

117

instance, when managers of a firm were also owners, able to claim the firm's profits — as was the case in the early DuPont company — their incentive to drive out internal slack was enormous. Motivated by the desire for personal gain, these owner-managers strove with single-minded zeal to use ·capital productively. Conversely, when a manager was not also one of the firm's owners, he could not be depended upon to husband the firm's capital resources.

MANAGEMENT ACCOUNTING IN THE MULTIDIVISIONAL FIRM

Organizers of large, vertically-integrated firms, whether those firms were owner-managed or agent-managed, might have turned to two market methods to achieve higher gains from capital (cf. Jensen & Meckling, 1976, pp. 328–329). They might have sold the firm itself in the capital market. Or they might have turned to a market for managerial talent to locate the best possible agents to run the organization. Immediately preceding and just after World War I, however, when large numbers of vertically-integrated firms first appeared in the United States, neither of those markets was well developed. Consequently, during the 1920s organizations searching for improved ways to use capital efficaciously created a new type of non-market organization, the multidivisional firm. The multidivisional firm generated within itself those two markets, for capital and for talent, which had not been provided by the existing market system (Williamson, 1975, pp. 145–148). The distinguishing strategy of those who organized multidivisional firms was to control a group of vertically-integrated enterprises through a non-market, internal structure. It was the structure of the multidivisional firm which made this control possible. And since such control would increase the returns from capital invested in vertically-integrated organizations, the structure supporting it was devoutly to be desired.

The structure, first, allowed rationing capital among divisions according to a criterion that reflected the organizers' concern for returns from capital, such as ROI. Second, the structure allowed

prompt removal of division managers who failed to husband capital satisfactorily. Although the capital market also possessed these monitoring and control features, nonetheless, it could not intervene in the affairs of vertically-integrated firms as precisely or efficiently as could the organizers of a multidivisional firm. The non-market structure, then, of the multidivisional firm allowed superior access to internal information and permitted swift fine-tuning adjustment. Thus, this structure provided managers with a stronger incentive than did the market to use advantageously the capital resources in their respective vertically-integrated divisions.

The resource allocation and internal incentive features of the multidivisional structure ultimately depended for their intended results, however, upon sophisticated and streamlined management accounting systems. The earliest and best-known management accounting system in a multidivisional enterprise, the one established by DuPont executives at the General Motors Corporation in the early 1920s, defined an immense domain for internal non-market search (Johnson, 1978). That well-known system linked every phase of the giant automaker's internal activities, future as well as present, to the organizers' ultimate ROI goals. The organizers' access to the internal accounting information made available through this comprehensive system enabled them to monitor precisely the efforts of each division manager. Furthermore, because accounting information embodied the ROI goal, it permitted organizers to ration capital and promotions among managers; in this way they intensified each division manager's search for better ways to fulfill that ROI goal.

Management accounting systems in multidivisional organizations (such as the one used by General Motors during the 1920s) accomplished the same objectives that cost accounting, budgeting, and other internal accounting procedures fulfilled in factories and vertically-integrated firms. They defined ·an internal, non-market domain in which search for gain was governed by the objectives of a firm's organizers. And they enabled organizers to intensify their search for ways to take every advantage of resources within that domain. But the management accounting procedures in a multidivisional firm also facilitated a unique kind of quest. The search for gain as it was conducted by organizers in factories and vertically-integrated firms focused simply on deriving the most benefit from resources in production processes or in raw material and consumer markets. However, the organizers of the multidivisional firm associated gain with deriving the utmost benefit from their treatment of other organizers; specifically, the managers of divisions. In this respect, the organizers of the multidivisional firm apparently fulfilled a role that neoclassical economic theory normally ascribes to the competitive market system itself (Williamson, 1975, p. 150), a role that the market system existing in the first half of the twentieth century seemed unable to perform *vis à vis* giant vertically-integrated enterprises. Empirical evidence seems to corroborate this belief; it suggests that multidivisional enterprises force higher returns from capital invested in internally-controlled, vertically-integrated firms than the market forces from capital in similar but autonomously governed firms (Armour & Teece, 1978). Evidently this is to some extent the case because management accounting information in the multidivisional firm imposes strict sanctions on management behavior, stricter than the sanctions imposed by market forces.

EPILOGUE

So far we have considered only how organizers' efforts to overcome market imperfections led to the development of accounting practice within firms. Another force that will undoubtedly influence future management accounting is the power of both markets and society to challenge the commanding position now held by large-scale firms in the American economy. A prognosis of future developments in management accounting must consider how markets and society may react toward organizers' efforts to widen the domain for search within firms.

Contemporary improvements in capital markets, for example, may someday reduce considerably the advantages enjoyed by organizers of the multidivisional firm. If future markets offer improved opportunities to search for, and select among, investment alternatives, then the multidivisional firm may diminish in importance, becoming very soon a transitory phenomena in markets and firms that, since the eighteenth century, have shaped management accounting practices.

Social and political pressures, moreover, may force management accountants to adopt a "commitment that transcends commitment to employer or client, recognizing the public interest to be paramount" (Brummet, 1980). A transcendent commitment to the public interest has not been a hallmark of management accounting practice, although the idea is not new. According to the noted German business economist Eugen Schmalenbach (1873—1955), accountants must recoil "from an identification of profits with . . . returns to the owner. The search for efficiency, economy and profits should not be of purely sectional interest." The management accountant, then, "should not be the lackey of the owner or the capitalist but must seek and measure social efficiency" (Forrester, 1977, p. 35). This concern to "seek and measure *social* efficiency" imparts an ethical foundation to the task of the management accountant. It invites him to employ internal accounting procedures to measure *all* the costs and benefits of economic activities that are conducted within non-market organizations. Such measurements would surely enhance society's freedom to choose among alternative economic opportunities — in both markets and firms.

119

BIBLIOGRAPHY

Armour, H. A. & Teece, D. J., Organizational Structure and Economic Performance: A Test of the Multidivisional Hypothesis, *Bell Journal of Economics* (Spring, 1978), pp. 106—122.
Baxter, W. T., Accounting's Roots and Their Lingering Influence, paper presented at the Third Charles Waldo Haskins Accounting History Seminar (Atlanta, 1979), 17 pp.

Brummet, R. L., The Societal Role of Management Accounting, *Management Accounting* (January, 1980), p. 4.

Chandler, A. D., Jr., *The Visible Hand: The Managerial Revolution in American Business* (Harvard University Press, 1977).

Chatfield, M., The Origins of Cost Accounting, *Management Accounting* (June 1971), pp. 11–14.

Forrester, D. A. R., *Schmalenbach and After: A Study of the Evolution of German Business Economics* (Strathclyde Convergencies, 1977).

Francis, A., *Markets and Hierarchies: Efficiency or Domination*, paper presented at the Markets and Hierarchies Conference at the Imperial College of Science and Technology (London, 1979), 17 pp.

Garner, S. P., *Evolution of Cost Accounting to 1925* (University of Alabama Press, 1954).

Gorelik, G., Principal Ideas of Bogdanov's 'Tektology': The Universal Science of Organization, *General Systems* (1975), pp. 3–13.

Hopwood, A. G., Editorial, *Accounting, Organizations and Society* (1977) pp. 187–188.

Jensen, M. C. & Meckling, W. H., Theory of the Firm: Managerial Behavior, Agency Costs and Ownership Structure, *Journal of Financial Economics* (1976), pp. 305–360.

Johnson, H. T., Management Accounting in an Early Integrated Industrial: E. I. DuPont de Nemours Powder Company, 1903–1912, *Business History Review* (Summer, 1975), pp. 184–204.

Johnson, H. T., Management Accounting in an Early Multidivisional Organization: General Motors in the 1920s, *Business History Review* (Winter, 1978), pp. 490–517.

Johnson, H. T., Toward a New Understanding of Nineteenth-Century Cost Accounting, *The Accounting Review* (July, 1981), pp. 510–518.

Landes, D. S., *The Unbound Prometheus: Technological Change and Industrial Development in Western Europe from 1750 to the Present* (Cambridge University Press, 1969).

Littleton, A. C., *Accounting Evolution to 1900* (American Institute, 1933).

Marglin, S. A., What Do Bosses Do?, in *The Division of Labour: The Labour Process and Class — Struggle in Modern Capitalism*, ed. by A. Gorz (Humanities Press, 1976), pp. 13–54.

North, D. C. & Thomas, R. P., An Economic Theory of the Growth of the Western World, *The Economic History Review* (April, 1970), pp. 1–17.

North, D. C. & Thomas, R. P., *The Rise of the Western World: A New Economic History* (Cambridge University Press, 1973).

Williamson, O. E., *Markets and Hierarchies: Analysis and Antitrust Implications* (The Free Press, 1975).

120

THE ROLE OF ACCOUNTING HISTORY IN THE
EDUCATION OF PROSPECTIVE ACCOUNTANTS

Being the sixth Arthur Young Lecture delivered
within the University of Glasgow on 22 November 1983

By

H. THOMAS JOHNSON

Director of the School of Business and Public Administration

The University of Puget Sound

Tacoma, WA   98416

U.S.A.

© H. Thomas Johnson, 1984

Published By

DEPARTMENT OF ACCOUNTANCY

UNIVERSITY OF GLASGOW

1984

THE ARTHUR YOUNG LECTURE

The University of Glasgow has instituted an annual lecture to be called The Arthur Young Lecture, financed by Arthur Young McClelland Moores & Co., Chartered Accountants, to enable a visiting lecturer of distinction to be invited to the University to give a public lecture on a subject of interest to accountants.

Research in accounting and related subjects is a very current topic of concern and it is important that the fruits of academic research should be related to and be capable of influencing the development of accounting practice. Effective communication between accountants and the professional accountancy bodies on one hand and academic researchers on the other is vital. The University proposes to devote this lecture series to this issue and in successive years to bring to a mixed audience of users, practitioners and researchers the results of current research.

THE ARTHUR YOUNG LECTURERS

1978	R. I. Tricker
1979	George J. Benston
1980	David Solomons
1981	Bryan Carsberg
1982	Athol S. Carrington
1983	H. Thomas Johnson

THE ROLE OF ACCOUNTING HISTORY
IN THE EDUCATION OF PROSPECTIVE ACCOUNTANTS

Abstract

The claim may be vigorously challenged, but it can be argued that accounting is not now a mature academic subject, and that it is not likely to become one until the study of accounting invariably encompasses the study of accounting history. The prospective accountant will eventually control his professional career, it may be claimed, if, and only if, he first studies how, and why, accounting has developed as it has. Once the student of accounting understands why, and how, accounting has evolved as it has, then he will be able to adapt with assurance to changing circumstances. Adroit and informed responses to changes in the profession presuppose knowledge of how diverse pressures in the past have shaped accounting.

In his lecture, Professor Johnson contends that the knowledge derived from research in accounting history should be an element in every student's study of accounting. By attending to the findings of accounting historians, one discovers penetrating explanations of the evolution of modern accounting thought and practice. Perhaps the essential conviction emerging from research now being done by accounting historians is the belief that the primary force shaping the development of accounting is the managed enterprise, a modern form of economic organization. Information about the affairs of the managed enterprise is indispensable not only to managers, but to society in general. Accounting grows and transforms to supply this information. The prospective accountant must learn, therefore, the dynamics of the managed enterprise and see how these dynamics create the need for accounting information. They must rely for this knowledge upon the work of those accounting historians, and also of those business and economic historians, who study the development of modern managed enterprise.

THE ROLE OF ACCOUNTING HISTORY IN THE EDUCATION
OF PROSPECTIVE ACCOUNTANTS

Introduction

Most accounting professors seem to believe that the task of preparing students to meet rapidly changing conditions in the complex business world precludes research and teaching in accounting history. Consequently they establish rigid requirements which virtually ignore the study of accounting history. This omission is profoundly ironic, for the study of accounting history actually increases an accountant's ability to adapt to change. It does so by forcing him to contemplate the causes of change in accounting practice and to project the directions dictated by change. If accountants understand why accounting has assumed its present shape, they are equipped to make informed judgments about the future of the accounting profession.

Knowledge of accounting's past helps one understand accounting's present and future because accounting is a technology. It is a social technology, one of many inventions of the human mind that result from mankind's relentless drive to shape, to describe, and to control his environment. Those inventions should be regarded, according to the late Jacob Bronowski [1976, ch. 1], as steps in the evolution of culture; the discoveries of any one era do build upon an inheritance from the past. Given this indebtedness of one age to another, it follows that we can comprehend the inventions of the present by studying their gradual emergence out of the past. Today's accounting students learn about accounting practice as though it solved problems in a vacuum. Accounting problems do have a historical context, however.

Markets, Traders, and Double-entry Bookkeeping

In the Western world, the historical context that gives meaning to accounting is the free market, an economic system for converting scarce inputs into desired outputs. A market provides those relationships between buyers and sellers which generate prices. Prices constitute information which decision makers must have in order to choose among opportunities for trade and exchange. Indeed, in the hypothetical world defined by neo-classical microeconomic theory, market prices provide all the information decision-makers need to allocate society's resources efficiently and effectively. In the real world, of course, the information provided by market prices is not always adequate. To illustrate how accounting serves decision-making, complementing the market price, let us consider the history of the market system.

The origins of our present market economy probably date from the eleventh century. Before that time, the basic economic problem of efficiently and effectively converting scarce inputs into output was solved primarily by small isolated social units such as the family, the clan or the local community. Custom and instinct provided these

isolated, small units with the only information they required
to select with discrimination from among the limited choices
available to them. In a few settlements around the North Sea
and the northern Mediterranean, however, people realized that
they could trade local specialties for desirable goods
produced in other regions. Taking advantage of opportunities
for gain, traders eventually developed those relationships
between buyers and sellers that we call markets. 127
Furthermore, their trading generated prices, and these prices
expressed the range of opportunities available for trade and
exchange. As markets expanded, occasioning an increase in
price statistics, economic opportunities increased. In the
Western world, the rights of the individual to the benefits
of economic expansion inspired an energetic and pervasive
search for efficient ways to generate, and profit from,
market exchange. That search has resulted, of course, in a
centuries-long rise in economic standards of living that
persists to this day [Johnson, 1983; North and Thomas, 1970].

The early merchants whose activities precipitated this
development are noteworthy for two reasons. In the first
place, these merchants anticipate those who trade in the
market system today, those who - by ceaselessly buying and
selling - cause each price to reflect the market value of
alternative opportunities. Only the countless attempts of
today's traders to "beat the market" make prices a reliable
basis for decision-making. In the second place, early

merchants are interesting because they had a penchant for bookkeeping. Modern double-entry bookkeeping actually originated between the thirteenth and the fifteenth centuries in such great centers of early trading activity as Northern Italy, the British Isles and the Low Countries.

It is not clear why double-entry was a popular bookkeeping procedure among early-modern merchants. One must be careful, however, not to explain early double-entry bookkeeping in terms of modern accounting concepts. For example, Sombart erroneously asserts, as Professor Yamey [1964] shows, that double-entry bookkeeping promoted the rise of capitalist enterprise. Sombart is not the only writer, however, who found in early double-entry books more portents of modern accounting than the facts justify. Others have also seen twentieth century accounting practices presaged in the books of Renaissance merchants. An interesting exception is a recent article suggesting that the double-entry technique emerged when it did simply because it gave persons in an arithmetically unsophisticated age a means to reckon with negative numbers [Peters and Emery, 1978].

Although we do not know precisely why early merchants kept books in double-entry, we do know why they kept account books. Before the eighteenth century, merchants kept books primarily because far-flung and time-consuming market exchanges stretched their capacities to remember and to trust. Merely to aid memory and, if necessary, to enforce claims in court, books recorded things owned, obligations due to, or from, others, and cash movements. Account books were not used before the eighteenth century to accumulate information conducive to economic decision-making. Since virtually all economic activities were conducted through market exchange, market prices provided all the information needed to assess existing opportunities for trade and exchange. Merchants did not require costly accounting procedures to garner information to aid decisions. Initially, then, bookkeeping was simply the keeping of records to aid memory.

129

Organizers, Managed Organizations, and Accounting

1. Conversion cost accounting in the single-activity organization, ca. 1780-1900

When merchants discovered that market prices do not always reveal the most efficient opportunities for conducting economic activity, bookkeeping evolved into accounting - the self-conscious production of information to aid decisions. This discovery was made in early eighteenth century England by those who stood to gain enormously from a pronounced rise in market demand for textiles [Libbey, 1973, pp. 216-218]. These traders became dissatisfied with the "domestic" or "putting-out" production system, a decentralized system of market exchanges that used continuous contracts and simple transactions to coordinate the work flow from raw material to finished good. Such a system made it difficult to increase textile supplies rapidly. Traders attempted in two ways to increase output. First they contracted with more and more independent artisans at each stage of production. Quickly they learned that the problems attendant upon coordinating large numbers of contractors inexorably drove up costs. Next they tried to entice more output from artisans by raising market piece-rates. Artisans responded, however, by diminishing output - a classic example of the "backward-bending" labor supply curve.

The question of how to increase output rapidly was resolved in the mid-eighteenth century mainly by merchants in the British Isles. They replaced the decentralized domestic system for producing textiles with a centralized administrative system, the proto-factory. The unique feature of this new centrally-managed production system was a wage contract between employer and employee. Unlike the piece-rate contract which obtained between artisan and trader in the domestic system, the wage contract empowered an employer to _manage_ labor productivity, thus enabling him to reduce the costs of increasing output in the short run. But an interesting effect of the wage contract is that a wage payment does not provide what piece rates provide automatically - namely, the information needed to evaluate labor productivity [Johnson, 1981, p. 512 and 1983, pp. 140-141].

A merchant dealing in the decentralized "domestic" system could refer to a market price - piece-rates - for the

130

labor productivity information he needed to judge alternative opportunities. The wage contract between employee and manager, however, did not allow the manager to infer information about productivity from the market wage rate. He therefore had to artificially synthesize this productivity information, and he did so by inventing cost accounting. By using accounting records to accumulate information about labor and other conversion costs, organizers of mid-eighteenth century proto-factories anticipated modern accounting [Johnson, 1983, p. 141].

131

Accounting students would gain considerable insight into the evolution and nature of cost accounting were they to analyze information contained in early factory accounts. Those accounts invite reflection about managers who used the information and the decisions they reached. Students would also benefit from identifying the many uses to which accounting information has been put by organizers of all kinds of managed enterprises, enterprises ranging from the earliest proto-factories to the latest multidivisional, multinational organizations. If they examine the historical development of the managed economic organization and of the accounting systems it generated, students would arrive at important insights [Johnson, 1975b].

The most fundamental insight afforded by familiarity with accounting's historical evolution is that it becomes necessary to account for decision-useful information when internal, managerial procedures are used to conduct economic activity. When managerial procedures are not used to conduct economic activity, as in a world of pure market exchange, market prices will provide all the information needed to make economic decisions. It is when limitations to pure market exchange give rise to managed, non-market coordination of economic activities that people need _accounting_ surrogates for market prices. As in the example mentioned above, limitations on potential textile output imposed by the market-coordinated domestic system encouraged the rise of the managed proto-factory and the concomitant rise of cost accounting.

Shaping the development of cost accounting during the eighteenth and most of the nineteenth centuries is the fact that a manager's chief concern was the efficiency with which resources were converted to output in fairly straight-forward, single-activity organizations. Managers needed accounting information to monitor the efficiency of conversion processes: cost accounting to provide labor conversion-cost data in factories; operating margin statistics to assess the efficiency of transportation activities on the railways; and inventory turnover statistics to assess the efficiency of space-using activities in retail establishments. One finds no evidence of systematic concern about depreciation. However, such an omission is not surprising in single-activity organizations, for such organizations permit directly assessing the efficiency with which capital is employed, without resource to accounting

132

data [cf. discussion of Carnegie in Johnson, 1981, pp. 515-516].

Of the refinements to cost accounting that occurred in the nineteenth century, two deserve special mention. One is standard costing, a refinement to factory cost accounting that in principle compares accounted-for cost figures with an outside "market" view of what ought to be a firm's conversion costs. We know that the earliest exponents of standard costing were engineers whose main interest was the practice of scientific management, not accounting as such [Epstein, 1978]. An intriguing question that no historian has answered is why accountants in the early 1900's resisted the eminently logical idea of incorporating standard cost information into the primary accounting records. Another quite different refinement developed in the late-nineteenth century is product cost accounting, the attaching of costs to products so that manufactured costs of products are deferred on the balance sheet until products are sold. The early factory conversion cost systems that I mentioned earlier had nothing to do with product costing. And as Murray Wells [1977] has demonstrated, the first writings on product costing were not by accountants, but by engineers interested in pricing and planning. Why product costing became the central purpose of cost accounting after World War I is another question historians have not answered. I contend that product costing in the twentieth century demonstrates what happens when accounting loses sight of it objective - information useful

133

for decisions.

2.   Management accounting in the multi-activity,
      vertically-integrated organization, ca. 1900

Following the development of conversion-cost accounting
in single-activity firms in manufacturing, transportation,
and retailing, the next major accounting development to occur
in managed organizations was the appearance of accounting
systems for planning and control in early twentieth-century
firms that integrated _several_ activities simultaneously in a
single managed organization. In approximately 1900,
organizers of certain firms that mass-produced manufactured
products discovered that one could _manage_ the flow of
activities from raw material to final consumer more
efficiently in a vertically-integrated organization than in
customary market channels. This discovery occurred primarily
to low-cost mass producers who could not trust wholesalers to
feature their product's unique traits and to lower its price,
or who could not trust suppliers of raw materials to share
scale economies made possible by the manufacturer's enormous
output. Such mass producers discovered that they could drive
slack out of market transactions, (to the advantage of both
their profits and customer prices) by combining
manufacturing, retailing, and supplying activities in one
managed organization [Chandler, 1977, Part IV; Johnson, 1983,
pp. 142-143; Williamson, 1975, Ch.5].

These producers wished to efficiently manage a diverse
array of activities that had previously been coordinated

through market channels. The organizers of vertically-
integrated industrial firms therefore developed accounting
procedures both for budgeting (both capital appropriation
budgets and current operations budgets) and for evaluating
performance within, and among, the organization's different
functional units. Among the accounting procedures that
provided decision-useful information in early-twentieth
century giant enterprises, perhaps none is more significant
than the use made of return on investment (ROI). ROI was
used as a common denominator to link budgeting with
performance evaluation (ie. planning and control). For
example, in the accounting system that the DuPont
organization was using by 1914, ROI gave managers a credible
surrogate for market price information, a surrogate they
could use to judge the efficacy of the firm's use of capital
at all levels in the company [Johnson, 1975a and 1983].
Accounting systems in many vertically-integrated
organizations today still apply this ROI criterion at the
departmental level to evaluate profit and investment centers.

3.   Management accounting in the multidivisional
      organization, ca. 1925

      The consummate use of ROI information did not occur,
however, in the centralized, vertically-integrated industrial
giants of the early 1900's. Rather, it occurred in the
decentralized, multidivisional organizations that appeared
just after the end of World War I. The multidivisional
organization is a managed organization that controls the

135

activities of a group of vertically-integrated enterprises which are known as divisions. The multidivisional organization surely ranks as the most sophisticated invention in the 250 year evolution of internal non-market systems for managing economic activities. Although the first scholarly analysis of the origins and properties of multidivisional organizations did not appear until 1962 [Chandler, 1962], at least 40 years after the first multidivisional organizations came into existence, countless academics now devote considerable energy to studying multidivisional organizations. They have discovered that among the many remarkable features of these organizations, one is particularly relevant to the evolution of accounting; namely, the use of ROI information to meter and to ration capital [Williamson, 1975, Ch. 8]. The multidivisional structure permits managers to use refined ROI accounting information to meter performance and to allocate capital among the organization's many sub-units. This accounting information provides a surrogate for market prices of capital which often reflects capital's true market value better than do prices available in the market place. One reason multidivisional organizations can offer more efficient non-market controls over capital than are provided by conventional capital markets is that superior information is supplied by ROI. The use of ROI in the multidivisional organization represents the culmination of accounting's evolution as a source of decision-useful information about the internal non-market

activities of an organization [Johnson, 1978 and 1983]. ROI
in the multidivisional firm imposes stricter sanctions on a
manager's use of capital than the market itself imposes.

This hypothesis is confirmed by empirical evidence.
This evidence, the result of investigations conducted in the
United States [Armour and Teece, 1978] and the United Kingdom
[Steer and Cable, 1978], indicates that a multidivisional
firm can force from the capital invested in one of its
internally-managed divisions returns that are higher than
those the market forced from capital in similar but
autonomously managed firms. Furthermore, these studies
indicate that the inadequate information formerly available
in capital markets imposed an exceedingly high cost on
attempts to discover the true market worth of investment
alternatives. That cost made it efficacious to employ
capital in managed organizations. In them, reliable
information was available to serve as the basis of decisions.

If in the future, improvements in quality and cost of
access to information in capital markets lower the value of
internal ROI accounting information, the scale and number of
multidivisional organizations could diminish. Such a
development may in fact be occurring now. Certainly in the
United States the rising number of divestitures, spin-offs,
and leveraged buy-outs reported every month implies such a
trend.

Study of the multidivisional firm gives students a
vivid insight into the symbiotic relationship between market

activity and managed organizational activity. One must understand this relationship in order to appreciate accounting's significance. When students examine the multi-divisional organization, they should consider why virtually all the accounting developments I have traced here - with the one exception of early cost accounting in textile factories - occurred first in the United States and only much later in other nations, most notably Great Britain. Evidently the relatively poor quality of markets and market information in the United States between the late eighteenth century and the early-twentieth century explains why many modern accounting practices emerged in the States. Americans pioneered the development of internal accounting systems simply because they were compelled to do so. Poor market channels prompted shrewd opportunists to devise internally-managed organizations that relied on accounting surrogates rather than on market price information. Great Britain's geographically-concentrated economic infra-structure, however, incorporating the world's most sophisticated financial services, market exchanges and transportation networks [Lazonick, 1983, p. 199], gave British organizers relatively slight incentive to internalize economic activities in the nineteenth and early-twentieth centuries. The imperfections in Great Britain's labor markets which did impede expansion of textile output, and ultimately did lead to the first discovery of factory methods for organizing production in the eighteenth century, was quite unique. As a general rule, however, British factory organizers faced very competitive markets for products, capital and non-labor inputs during the remainder of the nineteenth and the early twentieth centuries. I take issue, then, with those who claim that business growth requires strong personalities of the sort found in the nineteenth century American industrial scene. I propose, on the contrary, that poor markets, with their myriad defects, necessitate the development of giant enterprises.

139

Accounting To Investors: "Traders of Organizations"

Giant enterprises, encompassing a wide variety of economic activities, required accounting information useful to management. They also prompted the rise of investors, and investors demanded information which made further demands on accounting. Not until the late-nineteenth century did managed enterprises rely heavily for capital on outside investors. Investors became essential, however, as managed enterprises succeeded in internalizing enormous volumes of market activity by the beginning of the twentieth century in Britain and the United States.

One of the great puzzles in accounting history is why the information that accountants have supplied to investors in this century has been so very different from the information sought in the early 1900's by managers of many large organizations. We know that by 1920 many firms used internal accounting information on cash flows, on operating margins by segments of the business, and on ROI by activity center [Johnson, 1978]. With this information, investors could evaluate and compare one firm's internally-managed activities - the activities that give value to a corporation's shares - with those of another. While not perfect, these accounting signals probably afforded a reliable indication of a firm's earning power. Accountants in the modern age, however, have not provided investors with this kind of information. They have provided, of course, income measures that match allocated acquisition costs against so-called "realized" revenues. By virtue of this income measurement process, they have also supplied investors with balance sheets that reflect unallocated balances of net assets, not values. The information accountants make available to investors, prescribed by rigid bookkeeping procedures, frequently impedes evaluating the performance of a managed enterprise in relation to market alternatives.

It is, of course, delightfully ironic that about fifteen years ago professional accounting organizations enthusiastically welcomed a so-called new discovery - namely, that the main objective of financial accounting should be to supply investors and others outside a firm with information suitable for decision-making [American Accounting Association, 1966; American Institute of CPA's, 1970]. Has it not always been the objective of accounting to provide information useful to decision-making? Surely that objective is what separates mere bookkeeping from accounting. And yet, in the late 1960's, accountants responsible for preparing information for investors had to be reminded of that objective. The necessity is vivid evidence of how far so-called "financial" accounting has strayed from its real purpose in this century.[1] A fascinating quest for accounting historians would be to identify the events and the persons responsible for diverting financial accounting from decision-making and for identifying it instead exclusively with "generally accepted accounting principles."

Students become aware of the deficiencies of modern financial (ie. investor) accounting only when, having studied the so-called managerial accounting, they discover controversies regarding allocations, direct vs. absorption costing, and the like. Undoubtedly, most instructors explain these controversies merely by telling students that we account to investors as we do because the historical cost income determination model accepted by accountants requires it. But that model - matching allocated acquisition costs

---

[1] The first writer to remind modern accountants that the objective of financial accounting to investors is to provide decision-useful information was George Staubus [1954, Ch. 1 and pp. 112-113] in his 1954 University of Chicago doctoral dissertation, reprinted in 1980 by Arno Press. In a revised published version of that dissertation [Staubus, 1961], he went on to describe the criteria for evaluating the relevance and reliability of decision-useful information. The close similarity between Staubus' 1961 work and recent Statement of Financial Accounting Concepts published by the FASB deserves more attention from accounting historians than it has received. Historians should also pay closer attention to origins of the "decision-useful objective" [AICPA, 1970] that are suggested in a 1961 article by Justin Davidson and Robert Trueblood [1961].

and realized revenue - was merely a rationalization to justify a practice that began much earlier [Zeff, 1982, p. 49].

The origins of twentieth century accounting to investors probably reside in the account procedures that mid-nineteenth century British lawyers developed to settle estates and entities in liquidation. One wonders why these procedures became the foundation of twentieth century reporting to investors, when more enlightened procedures might have been emulated. Michael Mepham [1983] discovered just such enlightened procedures, for example, in the writings of the Scottish accountant Robert Hamilton. Accounting historians would do well to consider this matter of origin more attentively than they have. Why have so-called "professional" accountants in this century favored a model for reporting to investors that provides information largely antithetical to the accounting information that managers inside organizations produce for their own purposes? The twentieth century schism between financial and managerial accounting must seem absurd to any reflective accountant. Were students to understand the origins of that schism they might put in proper perspective controversy now engaging practicing accountants.

Future Prospects for Accounting

The study of accounting history also enables students to speculate intelligently about the future direction of accounting. Accounting will change, of course, and the causes of change will emanate from those economic forces that give accounting its _raison_ d'etre. Change will not spring merely from procedural canons that give accounting its form, from the pronouncements of practicing accountants. Rather, it will occur as a result of market conditions; specifically, the market conditions that change organizations' propensities to internalize economic activity.

143

Many internal and external pressures have certainly increased the efficacy of market processes in recent years. It is noteworthy, for example, that many of the world's largest and best known managed economic organizations are seeking increasingly close identity with their customers. They are, at the same time, striving to find measures of performance that identify the firm's activities, at all levels, more closely with market results. In part this "return to the market" undoubtedly reflects a defensive reaction to Japanese incursions into so many important markets. It also reflects a recent diminution of regulatory restraints on free trade within domestic economies, notably the United States and the United Kingdom. And, of course, the rapid spread of electronic communication and computing technology has suddenly increased access to information at much reduced cost.

What important changes in accounting might follow these improvements in market processes? In answer to the Japanese challenge, especially the challenge to raise the quality of manufactured products, some organizations are considering a shift from mass production to customized output. The technology exists to do this efficiently and effectively. Some authorities doubt that the cost accounting systems adequate to meet the needs of mass procedures can also supply proper information to manage this new technology [Kaplan, 1983, pp. 688-689]. One cannot say at the moment what answers accountants will provide. Students can surely, however, expect change.

144

Some changes in accounting practices prompted by the way organizations adjust to a competitive environment can already be observed. The key word I would use to describe these changes is "simplification." In organizations that alter their internal structures to become flexible and to respond to nuances of the market, managers are interested less in information from complex optimization models than they are in having direct market information - prices - to make decisions. Several interesting developments may follow from this:

1.   Current-value accounting, long debated and discussed, may become reality not because accountants finally accept the inherent logic in its use, but because improved market efficiencies make price information reliable, make it representative of market values [Johnson and Storey, 1982, pp. v-ix].

2.   Allocations of administrative overhead, formerly valued by accountants to garner cost statistics, will become valued by managers intent on making the most efficient and effective use of administrative resources. The principle being followed here - an old but often overlooked rule - is that market-responsive line managers who become mindful of the full burden of the firm's administrative overhead may propose interesting

and unexpected suggestions for reducing it [Blanchard and Chow, 1983].

3. Accountants' attitudes about cost will surely change when accounting cost information reflects market alternatives more reliably than it does now. Whereas managers in a regulated or protected environment lapse into the habit of viewing cost as a determinant of price, managers facing severe market competition view cost as something to manage – cost becomes a market opportunity foregone, not a Byzantine summation of outlays that customers inevitably pay for.

A more radical change than any I have discussed remains to be considered if the symbiotic relationship between markets and managed organizations outlined in this paper is true. This change involves the truncation, if not actual disappearance, of large complex organizations in the near future. Markets "learn" just as organizations do. Just as people often discover more efficient ways to conduct market exchanges by internalizing them in managed organizations, so also people discover more efficient ways to conduct market activity [Williamson, 1975, pp. 10 and 20-21]. Several developments described earlier are signs of the growing sophistication and increasing efficiency of markets in the Western world. Developments that improve the efficiency of markets will, ceteris paribus, raise the opportunity cost of managing in organizations and thereby reduce the share of economic activity transacted through managed organizations. Such a decline will mean that a smaller percentage of economic decision-making will rely on accounting information; more decision-making will rely on market price signals. Improved market channels may also lead to a decline in the

145

<u>size</u> of managed organizations, although that prediction cannot be made with absolute certainty. What does seem certain if market channels improve is that accountants in managed organizations will be expected to produce more and more information about internal activity performance <u>vis-a-vis</u> market alternatives. Thus, while present changes in the environment for markets and managed organizations do not presage an end to accounting as an important social and economic service, they may foretell an end to many accounting practices that accountants treasure, especially in the realm of accounting to investors.

Complementing these improvements in market channels is a growing concern among citizens of all free-world industrial nations with the social consequences of economic decisions. Here, too, is an area where questions and problems outnumber answers and solutions. I would suggest that students about to embark on accounting careers read David Forrester's eloquent discussion of the major works of the late German business economist Eugen Schmalenbach (1875-1955). Schmalenbach contended that the accountant "should not be the lackey of the owner or the capitalist, but must seek and measure social efficiency." To seek and measure social efficiency, the accountant must recoil "from an identification of profits with. . . returns to the owner. The search for efficiency, economy and profits should not be of purely sectional interest" [Forrester, 1977, p. 35]. Indeed, Schmalenbach was concerned that accountants should measure all the costs and benefits of economic activities that are conducted within non-market organizations. Schmalenbach's perception of accounting's ability to measure the social consequences of organizations' activities should be weighed by accounting students.

Conclusion

Many of my acquaintances, partners of international public accounting firms, are concerned about their ability to adjust to the rapid changes occurring in accounting. A similar anxiety is experienced by today's students. Professional accountants and students alike recognize that the extraordinary proliferation of rules and regulations may overwhelm them. This proliferation may be taking place mainly because accountants and too many accounting educators have been obsessed with accounting's form, as if accounting existed of, and for, itself alone. They have put accounting's form ahead of its substance.

Accounting's substance is the demand for information to make economic decisions about managed organizations. If by studying accounting history, students develop an awareness of accounting's substance, they will not be anxious about dealing with accounting changes. For they will understand the causes of change in accounting, and they will monitor developments in markets and managed organizations in order to anticipate change.

In so doing, perhaps they will even embark in a new direction. Committed to the idea that accounting's purpose is to measure the activities of managed organizations in relation to market alternatives, accountants may conceivably use accounting information in an unprecedented manner. Perhaps eventually they will use accounting information to judge the efficacy of all modes of economic organization in relation to the most productive modes known to exist. By enlisting the services of accounting in this very large domain, accountants might perform a significant role in assessing the need for change in a nation's basic economic system. Consider, for example, how accountants in this role would assess the productive systems in early-twentieth century Britain and late-twentieth century America.

On the one hand, Britain possessed in the early decades of this century a highly developed market system. Therefore British managers did not see any reason to adopt those large-scale managed organizations that were developed in Germany and in the States, enabling entrepreneurs in those countries to "beat the market" in several industries crucial to the British economy such as, for example, textiles, steel, petroleum, and machine-tool making [Lazonick, 1983, pp. 230-236]. On the other hand, although the United States, today, does possess some of the world's largest and best managed non-market organizations, nevertheless American managers are now failing to keep close to the market [Peters and Waterman, 1982, passim]. Some might argue that economic decline in

both Britain and America resulted because of entrepreneurial
failure [Locke, 1979]. In other words, those who ran things
concentrated assiduously on doing well with their present
system. Eventually, however, someone outside came along with
a new system. This different system permitted the outsider
to prevail. Can accountancy help us anticipate such changes
in systems, thereby giving us time to adapt? It is certainly
conceivable that a generation of accountants well-tutored in
accounting history might be able one day to make such
predictions. Perhaps this new generation of accountants will
become expert at what might be termed "entrepreneurial" or
"opportunity" accounting.

149

Rather than help managers and investors decide
how well organizations do in relation to _existing_ short-run
and long-run constraints, accountants might help them look
beyond those constraints and evaluate how well they _might_ do
using the best systems and practices known to man. If
accountants do not do this, their remissness may well
contribute to the failure of the free world's economy.
Obviously such a failure would leave us with nothing to
account for - in which case the _only_ thing left to our
accounting students would be the study of accounting history.

References

American Accounting Association (1966), A Statement of Basic Accounting Theory (AAA, 1966).

American Institute of CPA's (1970), APB Statement No. 4: Basic Concepts and Accounting Principles Underlying Financial Statements of Business Enterprises (AICPA, 1970)

Armour, H. O. and D. J. Teece (1978), "Organizational Structure and Economic Performance: A Test of the Multidivisional Hypothesis," Bell Journal of Economics (Spring, 1978), pp. 106-122.

Blanchard, G. A. and C. W. Chow (1983), "Allocating Indirect Costs for Improved Management Performance," Management Accounting (March, 1983), pp. 38-41.

Bronowski, J. (1976), The Ascent of Man (British Broadcasting Corp., 1976).

Chandler, A. D., Jr. (1962), Strategy and Structure: Chapters in the History of the American Industrial Enterprise (MIT Press, 1962).

Chandler, A. D., Jr. The Visible Hand: The Managerial Revolution in American Business (Harvard University Press, 1977).

Davidson, H. J. and R. M. Trueblood (1961), "Accounting for Decision-Making," The Accounting Review (October, 1961), pp. 577-582.

Epstein, Marc J. (1978), The Effect of Scientific Management on the Development of the Standard Cost System (Arno Press, Inc., 1978).

Forrester, D. A. R. (1977), Schmalenbach and After: A Study of the Evolution of German Business Economics (Strathclyde Convergencies, 1977).

Johnson, H. T. (1975a), "Management Accounting in an Early Integrated Industrial: E. I. duPont de Nemours Powder Company, 1903-1912," Business History Review (Summer, 1975), pp. 184-204.

Johnson, H. T. (1975b), "The Role of Accounting History in the Study of Modern Business Enterprise," The Accounting Review (July, 1975), pp. 444-450.

150

Johnson, H. T. (1978), "Management Accounting in an Early
    Multidivisional Organization: General Motors in the
    1920's," Business History Review (Winter, 1978),
    pp. 490-517.

Johnson, H. T. (1981), "Toward A New Understanding of
    Nineteenth-Century Cost Accounting," The Accounting
    Review (July, 1981), pp. 510-518.

Johnson, H. T. (1983), "The Search For Gain In Markets and
    Firms: A Review of the Historical Emergence of
    Management Accounting Systems," Accounting, Organiza-
    tions and Society, Vol. 8, No. 2/3 (1983), pp. 139-146.

Johnson, L. T. and R. K. Storey (1982), Recognition in
    Financial Statements: Underlying Concepts and Practical
    Conventions (Financial Accounting Standards Board, 1982).

Kaplan, R. S. (1983), "Measuring Manufacturing Performance:
    A New Challenge for Managerial Accounting Research,"
    The Accounting Review (October, 1983), pp. 686-705.

Lazonick, W. (1983), "Industrial Organization and Techno-
    logical Change: The Decline of the British Cotton
    Industry," Business History Review (Summer, 1983),
    pp. 195-236.

Lilley, S.   (1973),"Technological Progress and the
    Industrial Revolution, 1700-1914," in C. M. Cipolla,
    ed., The Fontana Economic History of Europe:
    The Industrial Revolution (Collins/Fontana Books,
    1973) pp. 187-254.

Locke, R. R. (1979), "Cost Accounting: An Institutional
    Yardstick For Measuring British Entrepreneurial
    Performance, Circa 1914," The Accounting Historians
    Journal (Fall, 1979), pp. 1-22.

Mepham, M. J. (1983), "Robert Hamilton's Contribution to
    Accounting," The Accounting Review (January, 1983),
    pp. 43-57.

North, D. C. and R. P. Thomas (1970), "An Economic Theory
    of the Growth of the Western World," The Economic
    History Review (April, 1970), pp. 1-17.

Peters, R. and D. Emery (1978), "The Role of Negative
    Numbers in the Development of Double Entry Book-
    keeping," Journal of Accounting Research (Autumn,
    1978), pp. 424-426.

151

28

Peters, T. J. and R. H. Waterman (1982), *In Search of Excellence: Lessons From America's Best-Run Companies* (Harper & Row, 1982).

Staubus, G. J. (1954), *An Accounting Concept of Revenue* (University of Chicago Ph.D. dissertation, 1954; Arno Press, Inc.,(1980).

Staubus, G. J. (1961), *A Theory of Accounting to Investors* (University of California Press, 1961).

Steer, P. and J. Cable (1978) "Internal Organization and Profit: An Empirical Analysis of Large U. K. Companies," *Journal of Industrial Economics* (September, 1978), pp. 13-30.

Wells, M. C. (1977), "Some Influences on the Development of Cost Accounting," *The Accounting Historians Journal* (Fall, 1977), pp. 47-61.

Williamson, O. E. (1975), *Markets and Hierarchies: Analysis and Antitrust Implications* (The Free Press, 1975).

Yamey, B. S. (1964), "Accounting and the Rise of Capitalism: Further Notes on a Theme by Sombart," *Journal of Accounting Research*, II (1964), pp. 117-136.

Zeff, S. A. (1982), "Towards A Fundamental Rethinking Of The Role of the 'Intermediate' Course In The Accounting Curriculum," in D. L. Jensen, ed., *The Impact of Rule Making On Intermediate Financial Accounting Textbooks* (Ohio State University, 1982), pp. 33-51.

152

Accounting Books Published by Garland

New Books

Ashton, Robert H., ed. *The Evolution of Behavioral Accounting Research: An Overview.* New York, 1984.

Ashton, Robert H., ed. *Some Early Contributions to the Study of Audit Judgment.* New York, 1984.

*Brief, Richard P., ed. *Corporate Financial Reporting and Analysis in the Early 1900s.* New York, 1986.

Brief, Richard P., ed. *Depreciation and Capital Maintenance.* New York, 1984.

*Brief, Richard P., ed. *Estimating the Economic Rate of Return from Accounting Data.* New York, 1986.

Brief, Richard P., ed. *Four Classics on the Theory of Double-Entry Bookkeeping.* New York, 1982.

*Chambers, R. J., and G. W. Dean, eds. *Chambers on Accounting.* New York, 1986.
Volume I: Accounting, Management and Finance.
Volume II: Accounting Practice and Education.
Volume III: Accounting Theory and Research.
Volume IV: Price Variation Accounting.
Volume V: Continuously Contemporary Accounting.

Clarke, F. L. *The Tangled Web of Price Variation Accounting: The Development of Ideas Underlying Professional Prescriptions in Six Countries.* New York, 1982.

Coopers & Lybrand. *The Early History of Coopers & Lybrand.* New York, 1984.

*Included in the Garland series Accounting Thought and Practice Through the Years.

*Craswell, Allen. *Audit Qualifications in Australia 1950 to 1979*. New York, 1986.

Dean, G. W., and M. C. Wells, eds. *The Case for Continuously Contemporary Accounting*. New York, 1984.

Dean, G. W., and M. C. Wells, eds. *Forerunners of Realizable Values Accounting in Financial Reporting*. New York, 1982.

Edey, Harold C. *Accounting Queries*. New York, 1982.

*Edwards, J. R., ed. *Legal Regulation of British Company Accounts 1836–1900*. New York, 1986.

*Edwards, J. R., ed. *Reporting Fixed Assets in Nineteenth-Century Company Accounts*. New York, 1986.

Edwards, J. R., ed. *Studies of Company Records: 1830–1974*. New York, 1984.

Fabricant, Solomon. *Studies in Social and Private Accounting*. New York, 1982.

Gaffikin, Michael, and Michael Aitken, eds. *The Development of Accounting Theory: Significant Contributors to Accounting Thought in the 20th Century*. New York, 1982.

Hawawini, Gabriel A., ed. *Bond Duration and Immunization: Early Developments and Recent Contributions*. New York, 1982.

Hawawini, Gabriel, and Pierre Michel, eds. *European Equity Markets: Risk, Return, and Efficiency*. New York, 1984.

*Hawawini, Gabriel, and Pierre A. Michel. *Mandatory Financial Information and Capital Market Equilibrium in Belgium*. New York, 1986.

*Hawkins, David F. *Corporate Financial Disclosure, 1900–1933: A Study of Management Inertia within a Rapidly Changing Environment*. New York, 1986.

*Johnson, H. Thomas. *A New Approach to Management Accounting History* New York, 1986.

*Kinney, William R., Jr., ed. *Fifty Years of Statistical Auditing*. New York, 1986.

Klemstine, Charles E., and Michael W. Maher. *Management Accounting Research: A Review and Annotated Bibliography.* New York, 1984.

*Lee, T. A., ed. *A Scottish Contribution to Accounting History.* New York, 1986.

*Lee, T. A. *Towards a Theory and Practice of Cash Flow Accounting.* New York, 1986.

Lee, Thomas A., ed. *Transactions of the Chartered Accountants Students' Societies of Edinburgh and Glasgow: A Selection of Writings, 1886–1958.* New York, 1984.

*McKinnon, Jill L. *The Historical Development and Operational Form of Corporate Reporting Regulation in Japan.* New York, 1986.

Nobes, Christopher, ed. *The Development of Double Entry: Selected Essays.* New York, 1984.

*Nobes, Christopher. *Issues in International Accounting.* New York, 1986.

*Parker, Lee D. *Developing Control Concepts in the 20th Century.* New York, 1986.

Parker, R. H. *Papers on Accounting History.* New York, 1984.

*Previts, Gary John, and Alfred R. Roberts, eds. *Federal Securities Law and Accounting 1933–1970; Selected Addresses.* New York, 1986.

*Reid, Jean Margo, ed. *Law and Accounting: Pre-1889 British Legal Cases.* New York, 1986.

Sheldahl, Terry K. *Beta Alpha Psi, from Alpha to Omega: Pursuing a Vision of Professional Education for Accountants, 1919–1945.* New York, 1982.

*Sheldahl, Terry K. *Beta Alpha Psi, from Omega to Zeta Omega: The Making of a Comprehensive Accounting Fraternity, 1946–1984.* New York, 1986.

Solomons, David. *Collected Papers on Accounting and Accounting Education. (in two volumes)* New York, 1984.

Sprague, Charles F. *The General Principles of the Science of Accounts and the Accountancy of Investment.* New York, 1984.

Stamp, Edward. *Selected Papers on Accounting, Auditing, and Professional Problems.* New York, 1984.

*Storrar, Colin, ed. *The Accountant's Magazine—An Anthology.* New York, 1986.

Tantral, Panadda. *Accounting Literature in Non-Accounting Journals: An Annotated Bibliography.* New York, 1984.

*Vangermeersch, Richard, ed. *The Contributions of Alexander Hamilton Church to Accounting and Management.* New York, 1986.

*Vangermeersch, Richard, ed. *Financial Accounting Milestones in the Annual Reports of United States Steel Corporation—The First Seven Decades.* New York, 1986.

Whitmore, John. *Factory Accounts.* New York, 1984.

Yamey, Basil S. *Further Essays on the History of Accounting.* New York, 1982.

Zeff, Stephen A., ed. *The Accounting Postulates and Principles Controversy of the 1960s.* New York, 1982.

Zeff, Stephen A., ed. *Accounting Principles Through the Years: The Views of Professional and Academic Leaders 1938–1954.* New York, 1982.

Zeff, Stephen A., and Maurice Moonitz, eds. *Sourcebook on Accounting Principles and Auditing Procedures: 1917–1953 (in two volumes).* New York, 1984.

Reprinted Titles

American Institute of Accountants. *Fiftieth Anniversary Celebration.* Chicago, 1937 (Garland reprint, 1982).

American Institute of Accountants. *Library Catalogue.* New York, 1919 (Garland reprint, 1982).

Arthur Andersen Company. *The First Fifty Years 1913–1963.* Chicago, 1963 (Garland reprint, 1984).

*Bevis, Herman W. *Corporate Financial Reporting in a Competitive Economy.* New York, 1965 (Garland reprint, 1986).

*Bonini, Charles P., Robert K. Jaedicke, and Harvey M. Wagner, eds. *Management Controls: New Directions in Basic Research.* New York, 1964 (Garland reprint, 1986).

Bray, F. Sewell. *Four Essays in Accounting Theory*. London, 1953. *Bound with* Institute of Chartered Accountants in England and Wales and the National Institute of Economic and Social Research. *Some Accounting Terms and Concepts*. Cambridge, 1951 (Garland reprint, 1982).

Brown, R. Gene, and Kenneth S. Johnston. *Paciolo on Accounting*. New York, 1963 (Garland reprint, 1984).

*Carey, John L., and William O. Doherty, eds. *Ethical Standards of the Accounting Profession*. New York, 1966 (Garland reprint, 1986).

Chambers, R. J. *Accounting in Disarray*. Melbourne, 1973 (Garland reprint, 1982).

Cooper, Ernest. *Fifty-seven Years in an Accountant's Office. See* Sir Russell Kettle.

Couchman, Charles B. *The Balance-Sheet*. New York, 1924 (Garland reprint, 1982).

Couper, Charles Tennant. *Report of the Trial . . . Against the Directors and Manager of the City of Glasgow Bank*. Edinburgh, 1879 (Garland reprint, 1984).

Cutforth, Arthur E. *Audits*. London, 1906 (Garland reprint, 1982).

Cutforth, Arthur E. *Methods of Amalgamation*. London, 1926 (Garland reprint, 1982).

Deinzer, Harvey T. *Development of Accounting Thought*. New York, 1965 (Garland reprint, 1984).

De Paula, F.R.M. *The Principles of Auditing*. London, 1915 (Garland reprint, 1984).

Dickerson, R. W. *Accountants and the Law of Negligence*. Toronto, 1966 (Garland reprint, 1982).

Dodson, James. *The Accountant, or, the Method of Bookkeeping Deduced from Clear Principles, and Illustrated by a Variety of Examples*. London, 1750 (Garland reprint, 1984).

Dyer, S. *A Common Sense Method of Double Entry Bookkeeping, on First Principles, as Suggested by De Morgan. Part I, Theoretical*. London, 1897 (Garland reprint, 1984).

*The Fifth International Congress on Accounting, 1938 {Kongress-Archiv 1938 des V. Internationalen Prüfungs- und Treuhand-Kongresses}. Berlin, 1938 (Garland reprint, 1986).

Finney, H. A. Consolidated Statements. New York, 1922 (Garland reprint, 1982).

Fisher, Irving. The Rate of Interest. New York, 1907 (Garland reprint, 1982).

Florence, P. Sargant. Economics of Fatigue of Unrest and the Efficiency of Labour in English and American Industry. London, 1923 (Garland reprint, 1984).

Fourth International Congress on Accounting 1933. London, 1933 (Garland reprint, 1982).

Foye, Arthur B. Haskins & Sells: Our First Seventy-Five Years. New York, 1970 (Garland reprint, 1984).

Garnsey, Sir Gilbert. Holding Companies and Their Published Accounts. London, 1923. Bound with Sir Gilbert Garnsey. Limitations of a Balance Sheet. London, 1928 (Garland reprint, 1982).

Garrett, A. A. The History of the Society of Incorporated Accountants, 1885–1957. Oxford, 1961 (Garland reprint, 1984).

Gilman, Stephen. Accounting Concepts of Profit. New York, 1939 (Garland reprint, 1982).

*Gordon, William. The Universal Accountant, and Complete Merchant . . . [Volume II]. Edinburgh, 1765 (Garland reprint, 1986).

*Green, Wilmer. History and Survey of Accountancy. Brooklyn, 1930 (Garland reprint, 1986).

Hamilton, Robert. An Introduction to Merchandise, Parts IV and V (Italian Bookkeeping and Practical Bookkeeping). Edinburgh, 1788 (Garland reprint, 1982).

Hatton, Edward. The Merchant's Magazine: or, Trades-man's Treasury. London, 1695 (Garland reprint, 1982).

Hills, George S. The Law of Accounting and Financial Statements. Boston, 1957 (Garland reprint, 1982).

*A History of Cooper Brothers & Co. 1854 to 1954. London, 1954 (Garland reprint, 1986).

Hofstede, Geert. The Game of Budget Control. Assen, 1967 (Garland reprint, 1984).

Howitt, Sir Harold. The History of The Institute of Chartered Accountants in England and Wales 1880–1965, and of Its Founder Accountancy Bodies 1870–1880. London, 1966 (Garland reprint, 1984).

Institute of Chartered Accountants in England and Wales and The National Institute of Economic and Social Research. Some Accounting Terms and Concepts. See F. Sewell Bray.

Institute of Chartered Accountants of Scotland. History of the Chartered Accountants of Scotland from the Earliest Times to 1954. Edinburgh, 1954 (Garland reprint, 1984).

International Congress on Accounting 1929. New York, 1930 (Garland reprint, 1982).

*Jaedicke, Robert K., Yuji Ijiri, and Oswald Nielsen, eds. Research in Accounting Measurement. American Accounting Association, 1966 (Garland reprint, 1986).

Keats, Charles. Magnificent Masquerade. New York, 1964 (Garland reprint, 1982).

Kettle, Sir Russell. Deloitte & Co. 1845–1956. Oxford, 1958. Bound with Ernest Cooper. Fifty-seven Years in an Accountant's Office. London, 1921 (Garland reprint, 1982).

Kitchen, J., and R. H. Parker. Accounting Thought and Education: Six English Pioneers. London, 1980 (Garland reprint, 1984).

Lacey, Kenneth. Profit Measurement and Price Changes. London, 1952 (Garland reprint, 1982).

Lee, Chauncey. The American Accomptant. Lansingburgh, 1797 (Garland reprint, 1982).

Lee, T. A., and R. H. Parker. The Evolution of Corporate Financial Reporting. Middlesex, 1979 (Garland reprint, 1984).

*Malcolm, Alexander. A Treatise of Book-Keeping, or, Merchants Accounts; In the Italian Method of Debtor and Creditor; Wherein the Fundamental Principles of That Curious and Approved Method Are Clearly and Fully Explained and Demonstrated . . . To Which Are Added, Instructions for Gentlemen of Land Estates, and Their Stewards or Factors: With Directions Also for Retailers, and Other More Private Persons. London, 1731 (Garland reprint, 1986).

*Meij, J. L., ed. Depreciation and Replacement Policy. Chicago, 1961 (Garland reprint, 1986).

Newlove, George Hills. Consolidated Balance Sheets. New York, 1926 (Garland reprint, 1982).

*North, Roger. The Gentleman Accomptant; or, An Essay to Unfold the Mystery of Accompts; By Way of Debtor and Creditor, Commonly Called Merchants Accompts, and Applying the Same to the Concerns of the Nobility and Gentry of England. London, 1714 (Garland reprint, 1986).

Pryce-Jones, Janet E., and R. H. Parker. Accounting in Scotland: A Historical Bibliography. Edinburgh, 1976 (Garland reprint, 1984).

Robinson, H. W. A History of Accountants in Ireland. Dublin, 1964 (Garland reprint, 1984).

Robson, T. B. Consolidated and Other Group Accounts. London, 1950 (Garland reprint, 1982).

Rorem, C. Rufus. Accounting Method. Chicago, 1928 (Garland reprint, 1982).

*Saliers, Earl A., ed. Accountants' Handbook. New York, 1923 (Garland reprint, 1986).

Samuel, Horace B. Shareholder's Money. London, 1933 (Garland reprint, 1982).

The Securities and Exchange Commission in the Matter of McKesson & Robbins, Inc. Report on Investigation. Washington, D.C., 1940 (Garland reprint, 1982).

The Securities and Exchange Commission in the Matter of McKesson & Robbins, Inc. Testimony of Expert Witnesses. Washington, D.C., 1939 (Garland reprint, 1982).

*Shaplen, Robert. Kreuger: Genius and Swindler. New York, 1960 (Garland reprint, 1986).

Singer, H. W. *Standardized Accountancy in Germany. (With a new appendix.)* Cambridge, 1943 (*Garland reprint, 1982*).

The Sixth International Congress on Accounting. London, 1952 (Garland reprint, 1984).

*Stewart, Jas. C. (with a new introductory note by T. A. Lee). *Pioneers of a Profession: Chartered Accountants to 1879.* Edinburgh, 1977 (Garland reprint, 1986).

Thompson, Wardbaugh. *The Accomptant's Oracle: or, Key to Science, Being a Compleat Practical System of Book-keeping.* York, 1777 (Garland reprint, 1984).

*Vatter, William J. *Managerial Accounting.* New York, 1950 (Garland reprint, 1986).

*Woolf, Arthur H. *A Short History of Accountants and Accountancy.* London, 1912 (Garland reprint, 1986).

Yamey, B. S., H. C. Edey, and Hugh W. Thomson. *Accounting in England and Scotland: 1543–1800.* London, 1963 (Garland reprint, 1982).